MEDIEVAL
Fantasy
Coloring Book For All Ages

illustrated by
Rachel Jones

FREE BONUS PAGES

Visit: http://racheljonesarts.com/medieval-fantasy/ to receive a PDF of 5 bonus coloring pages.

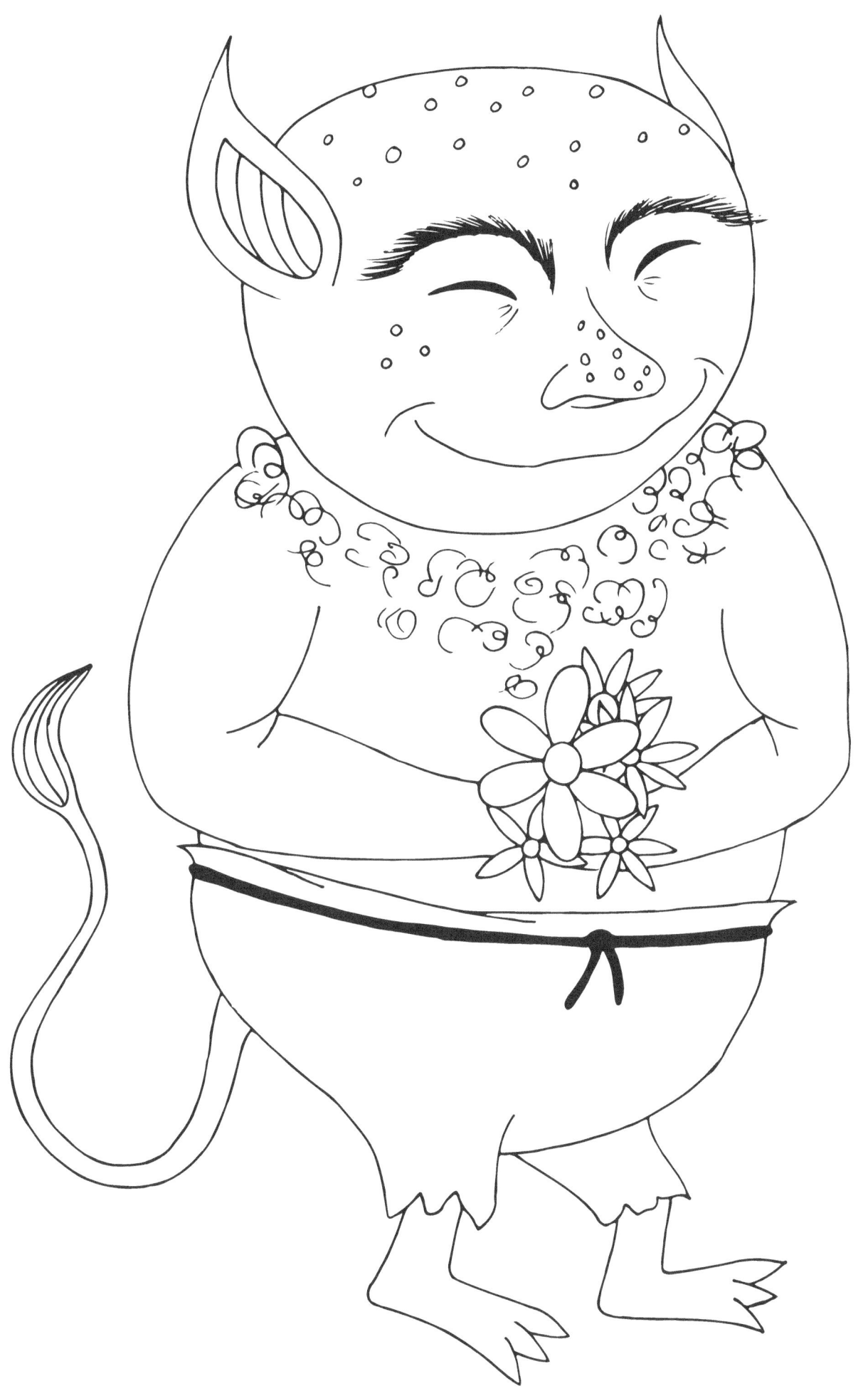

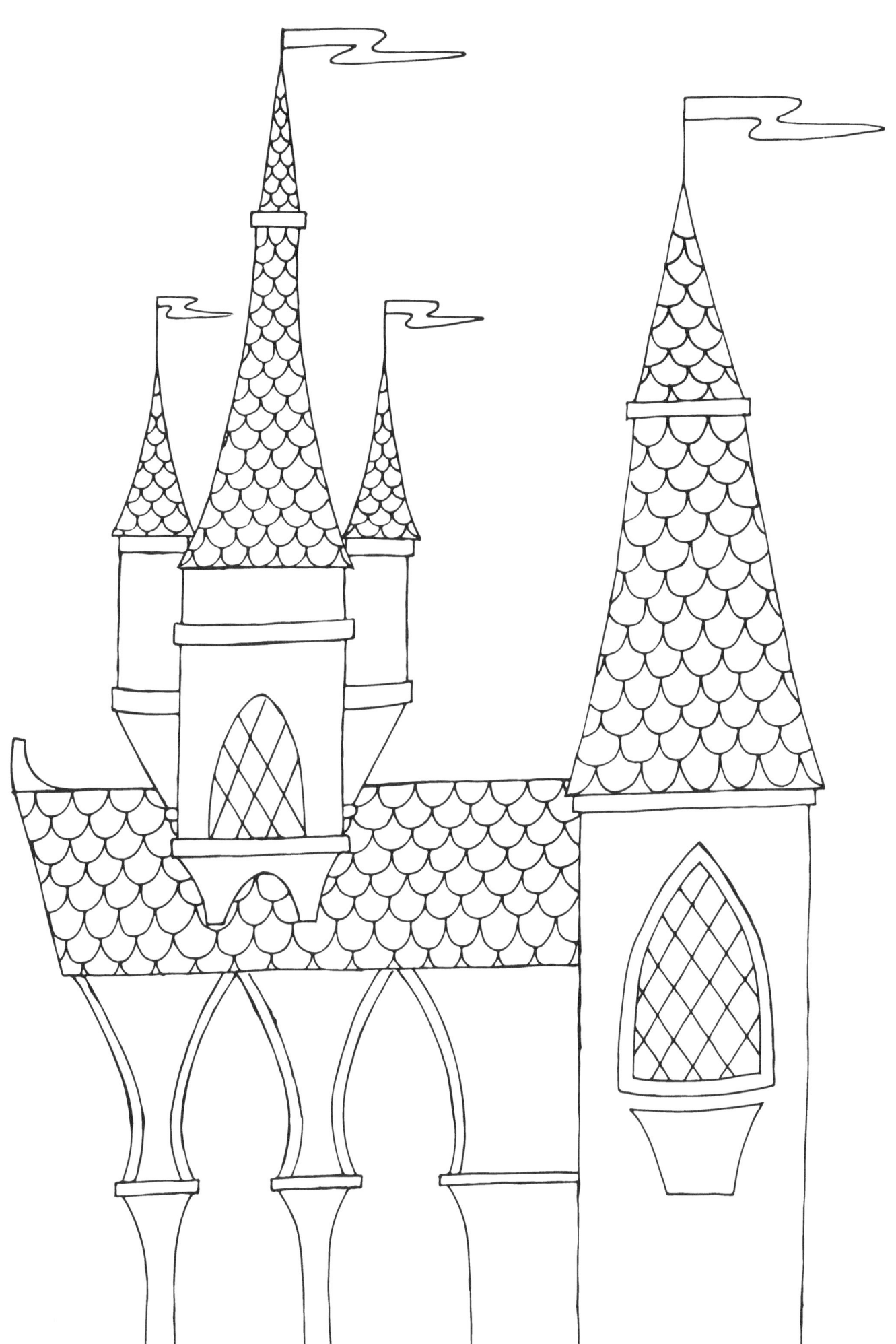

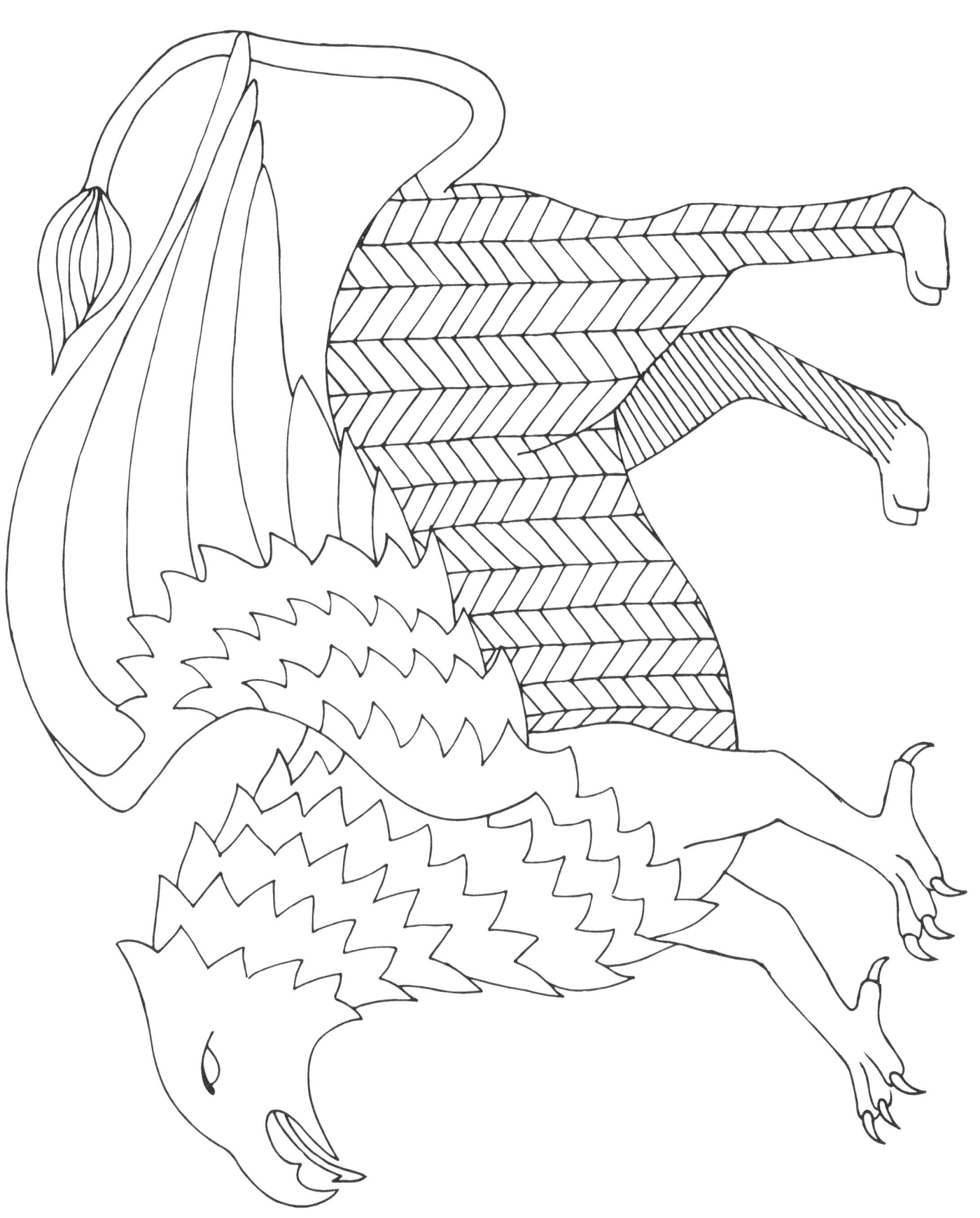

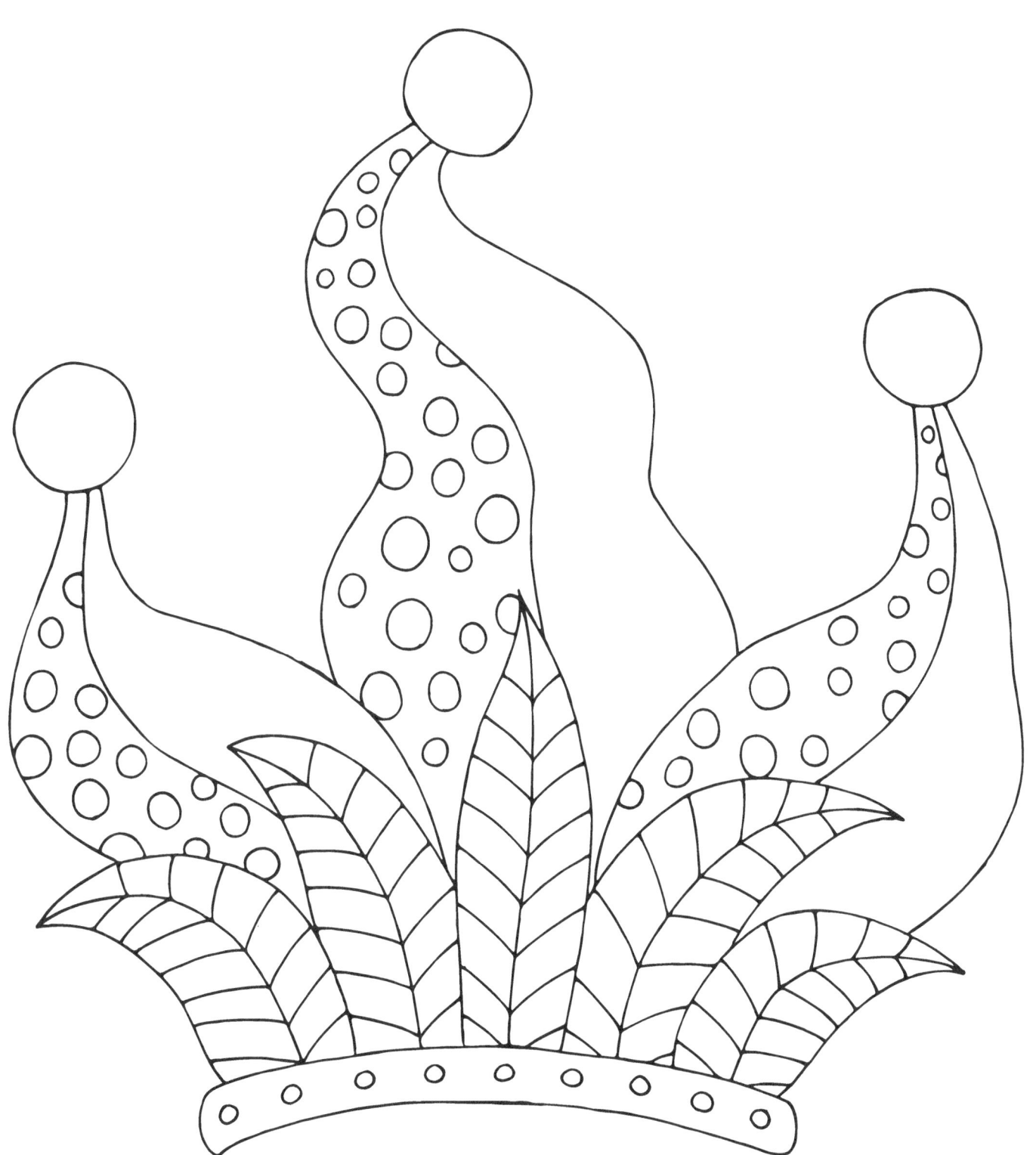

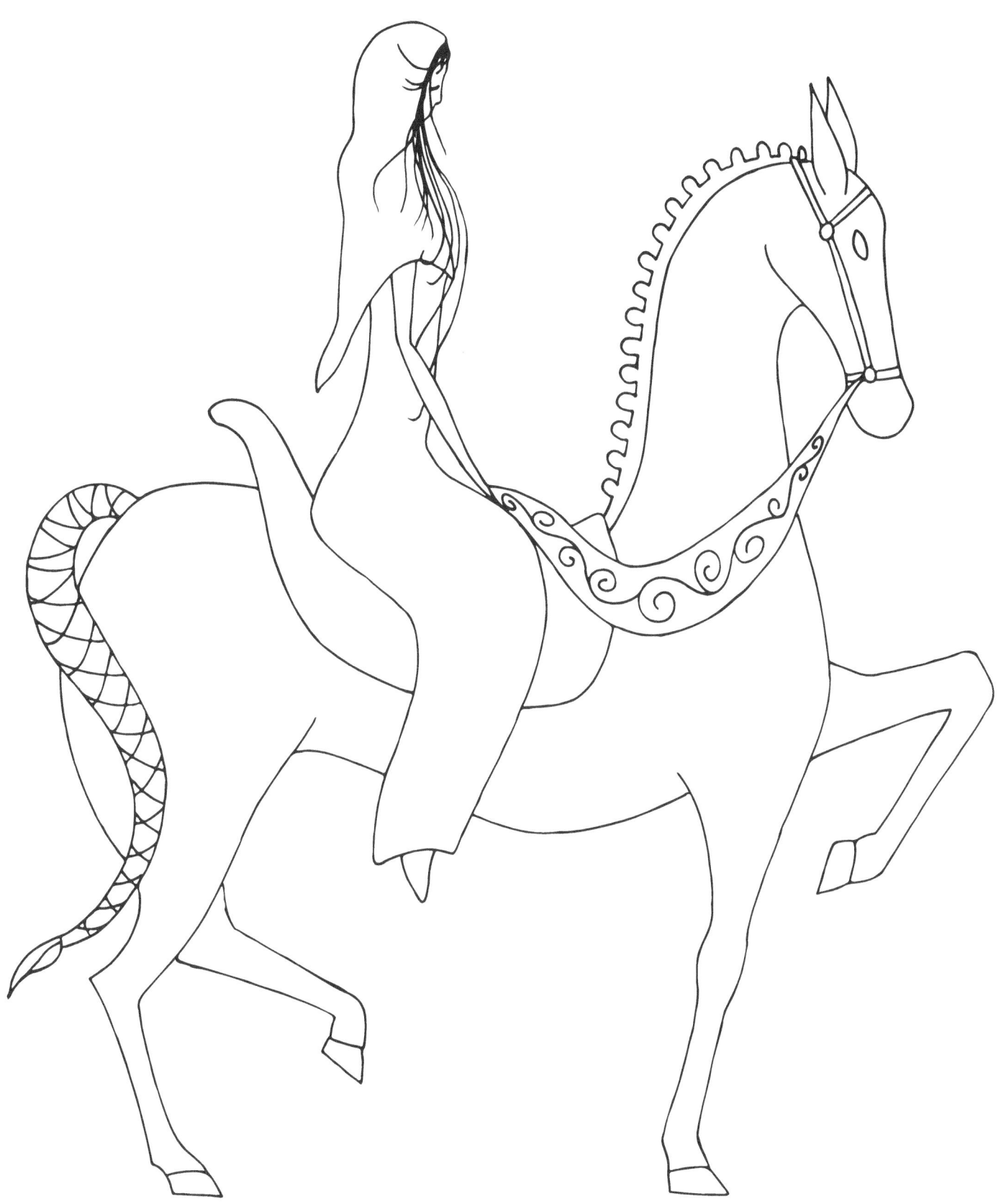

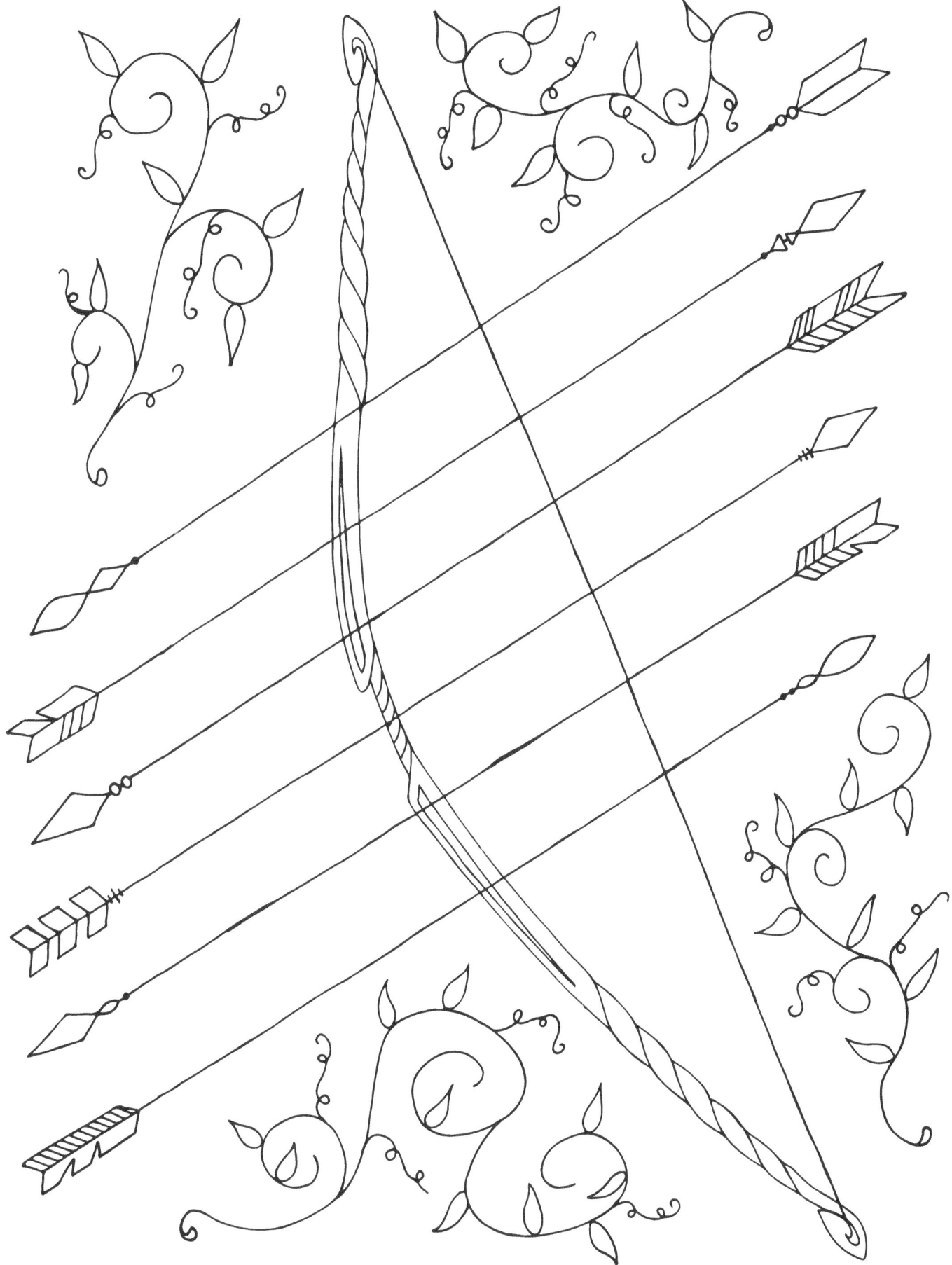

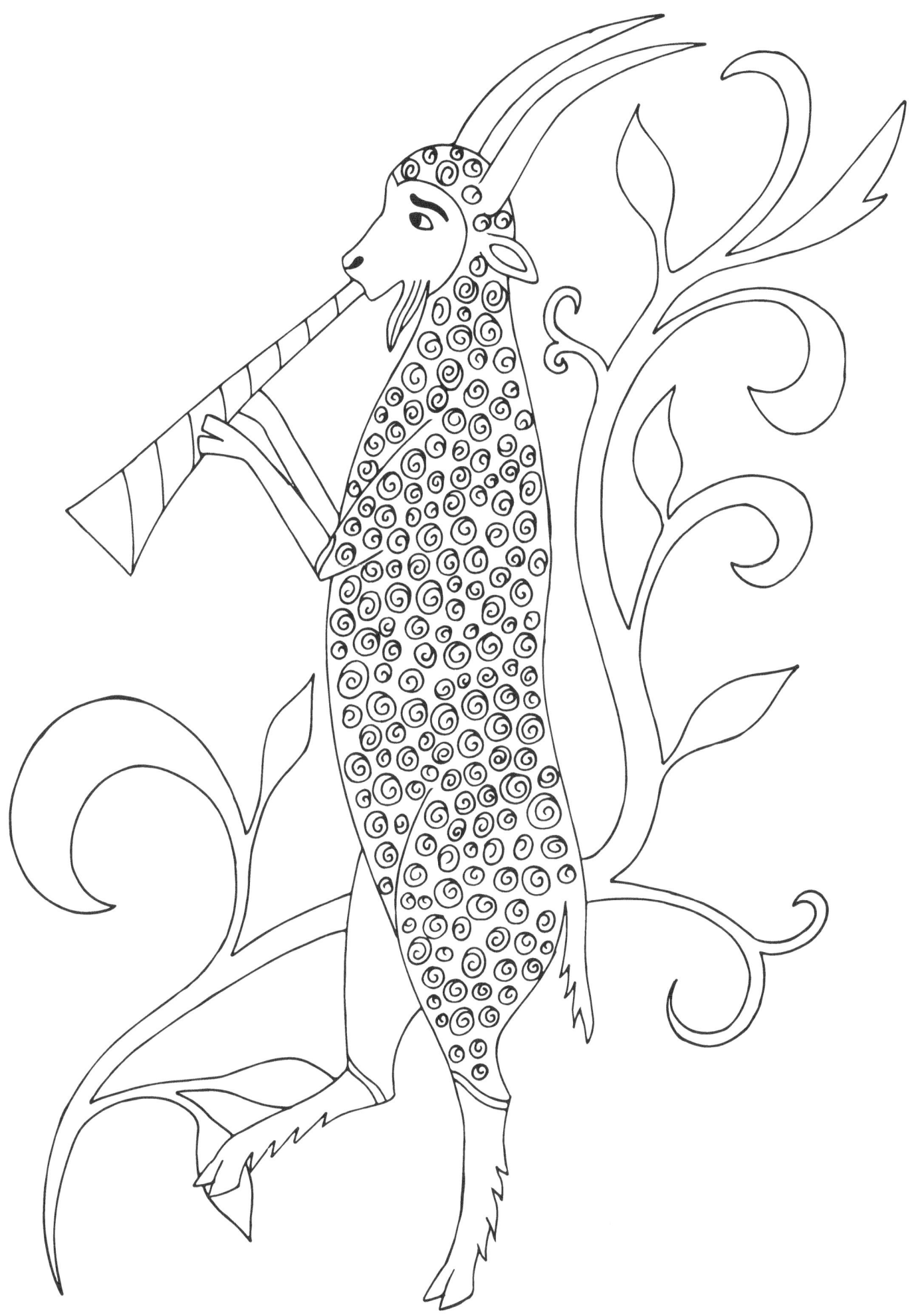

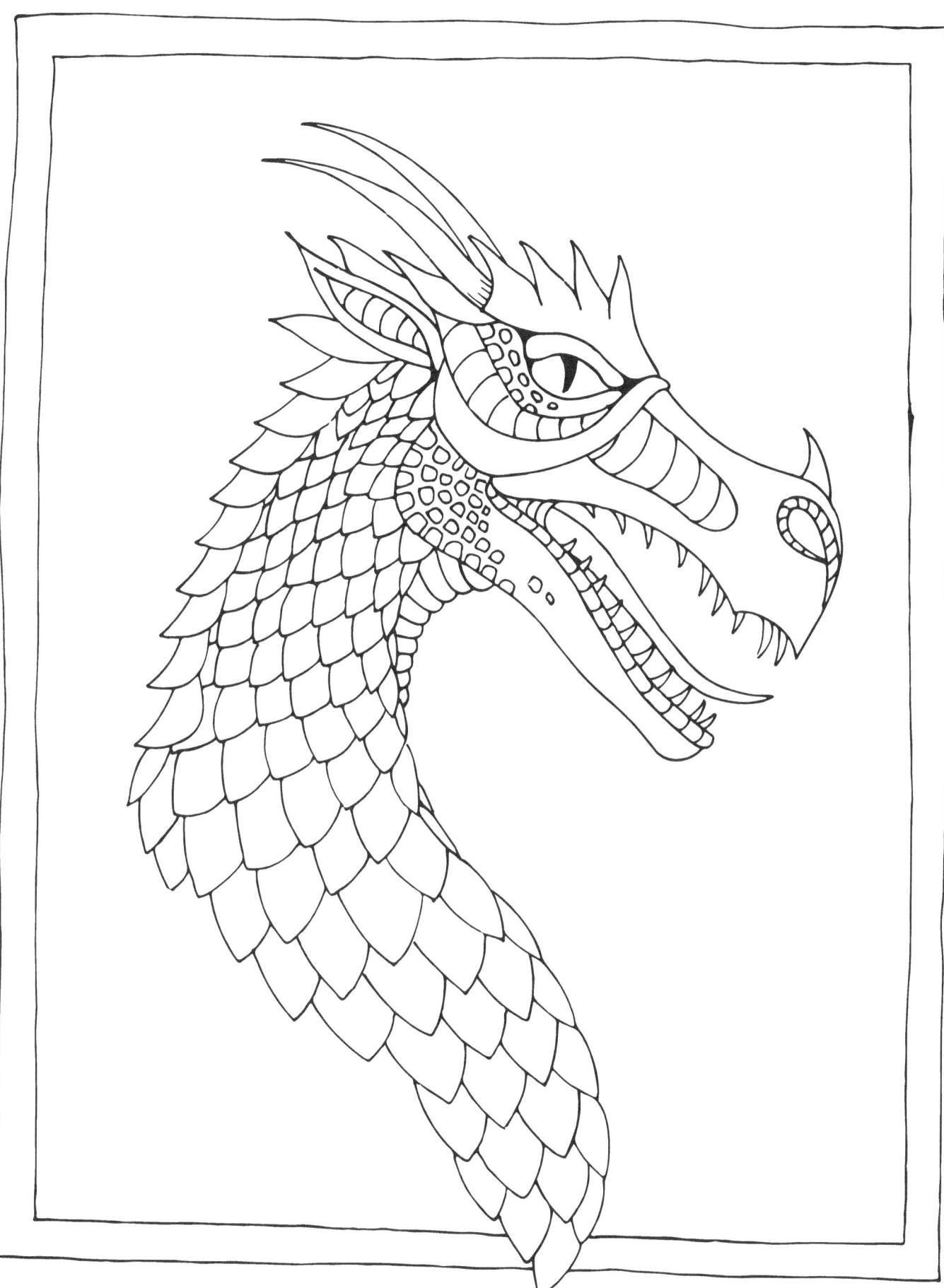

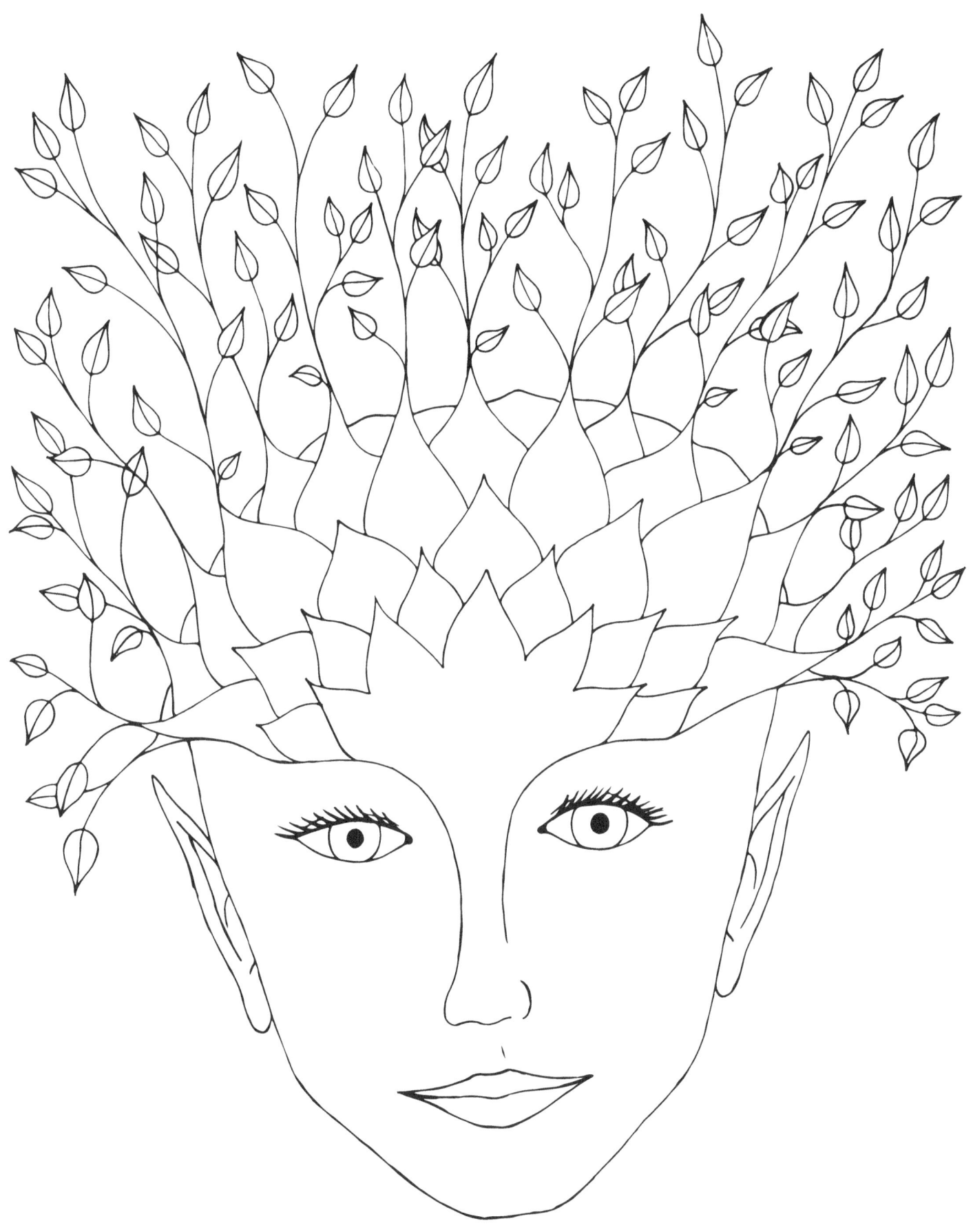

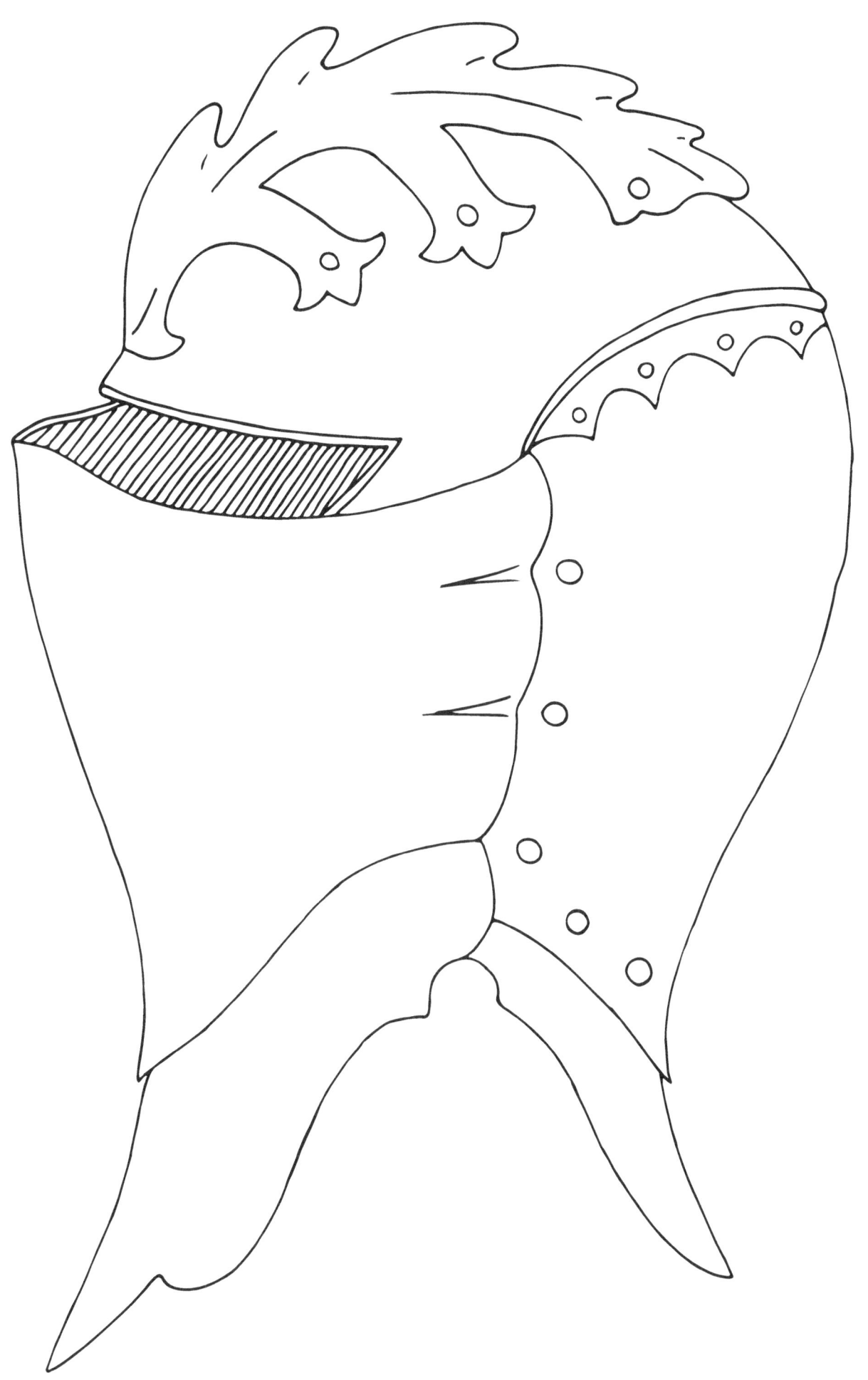

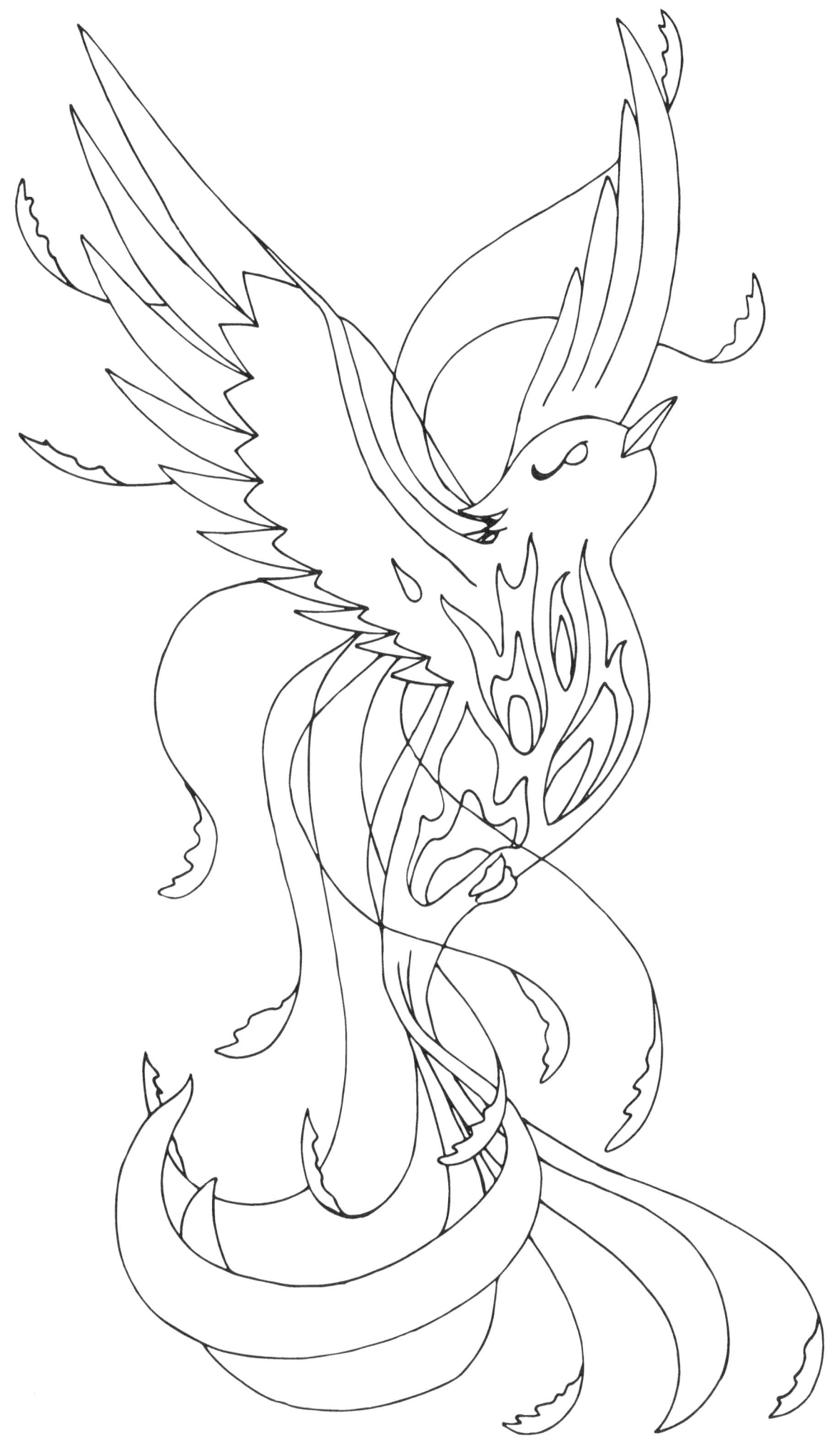

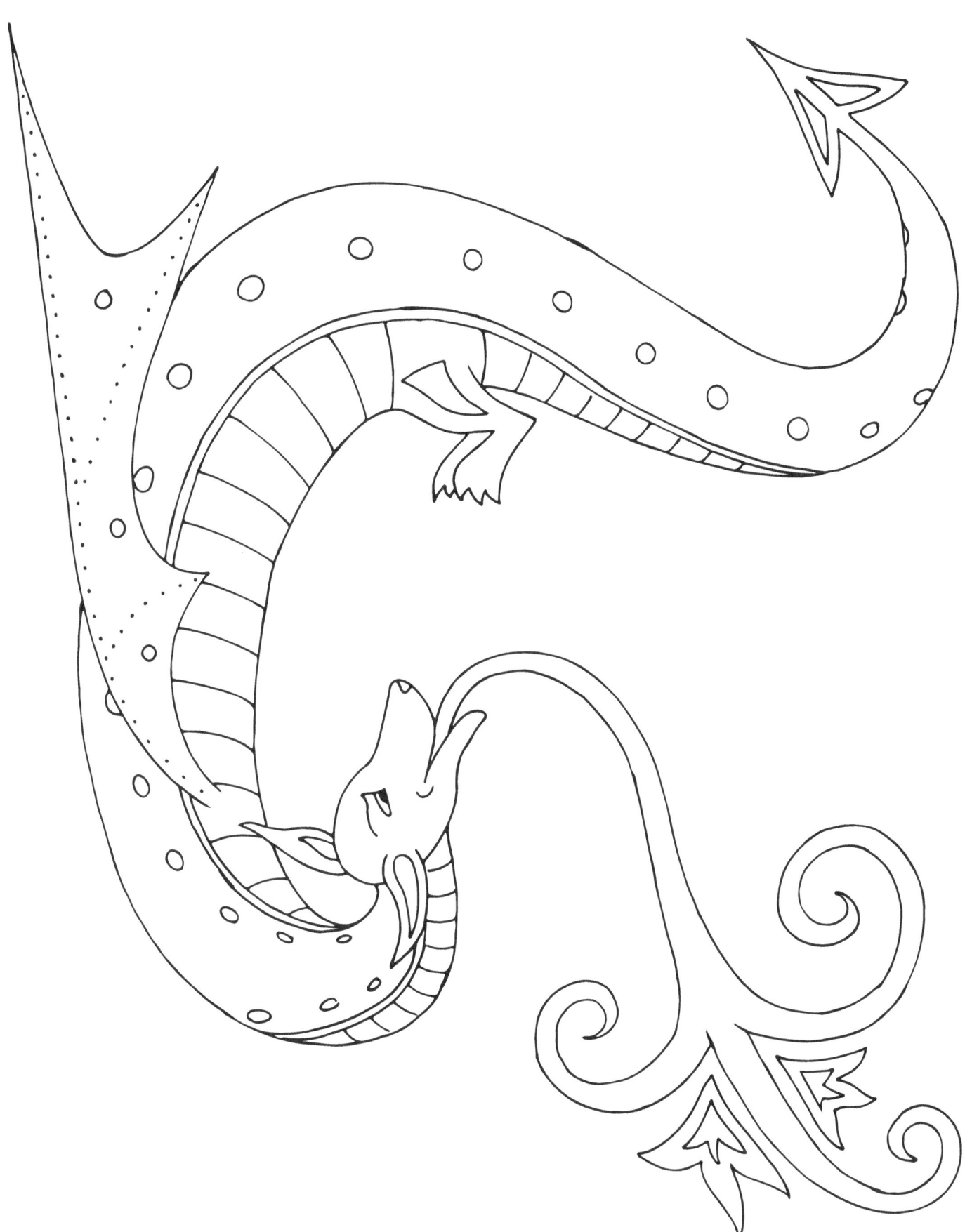

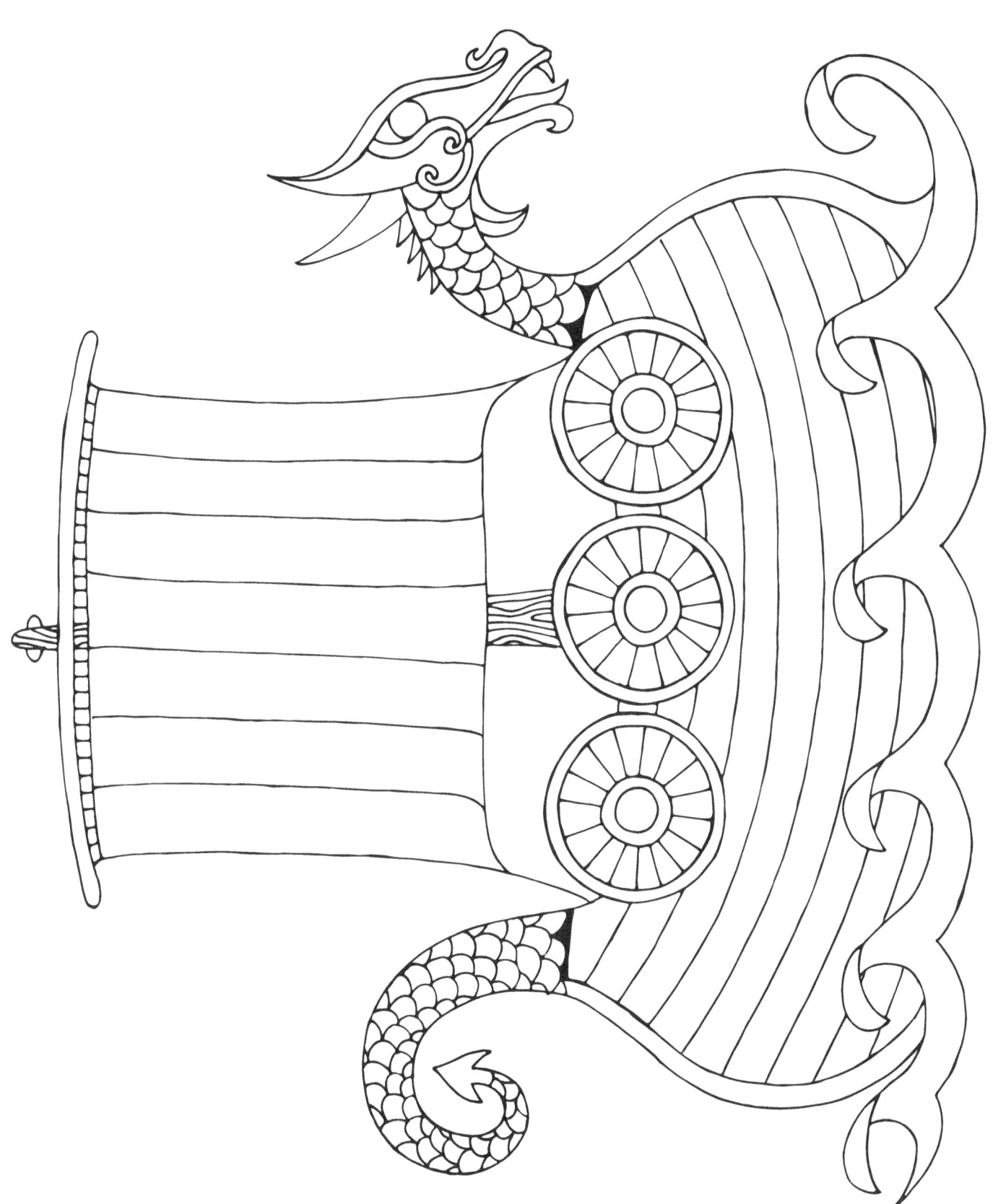

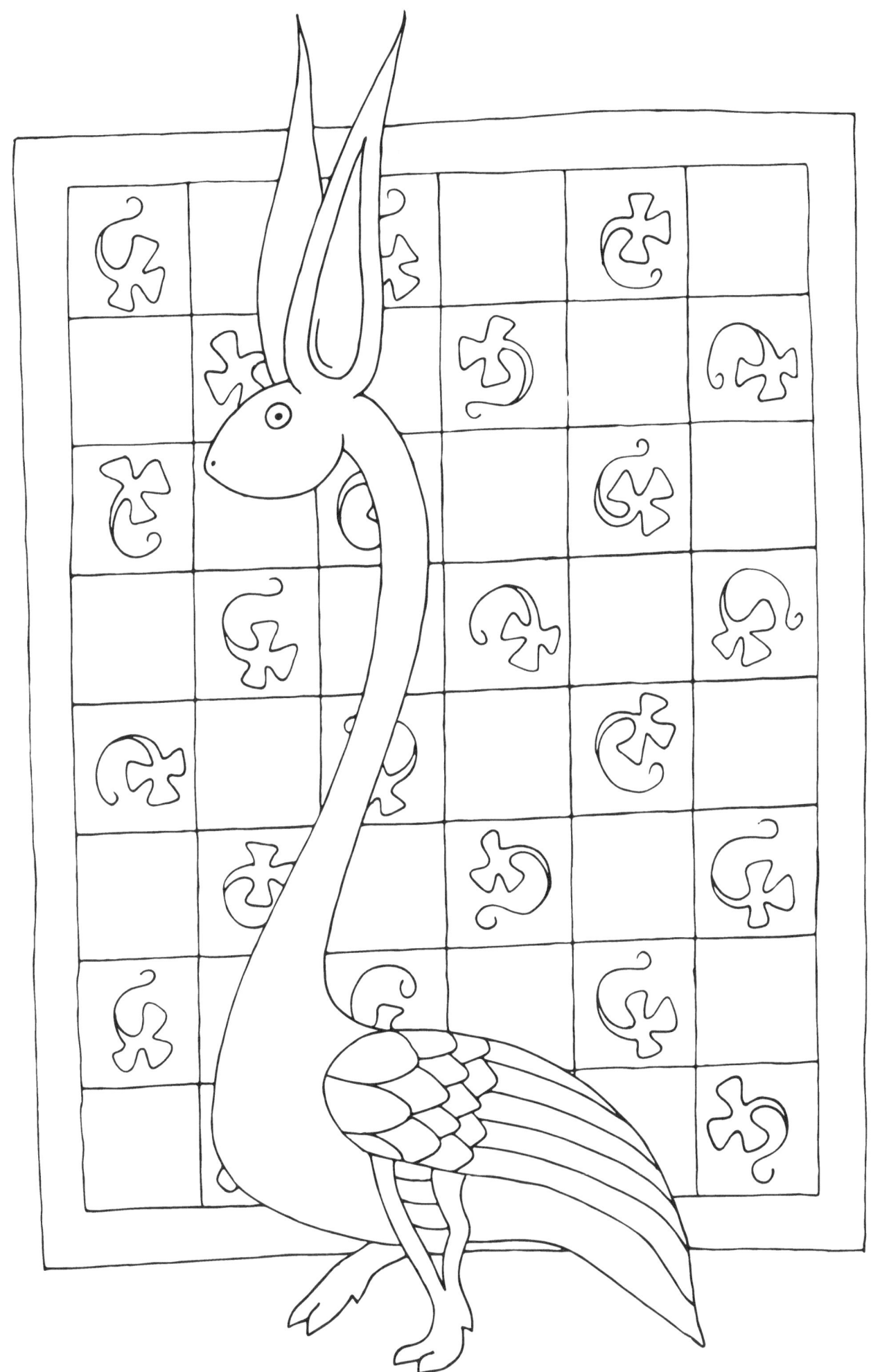

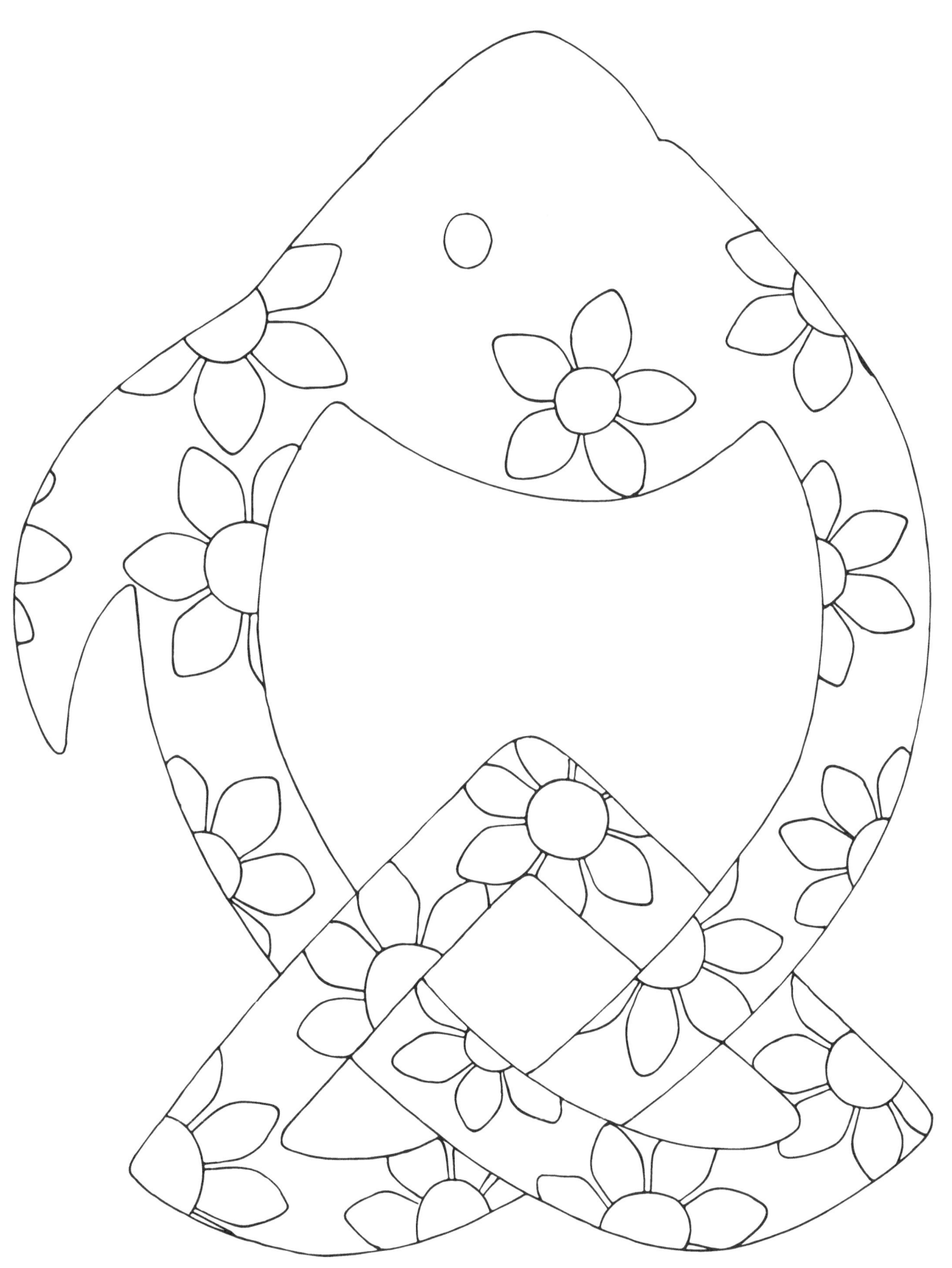

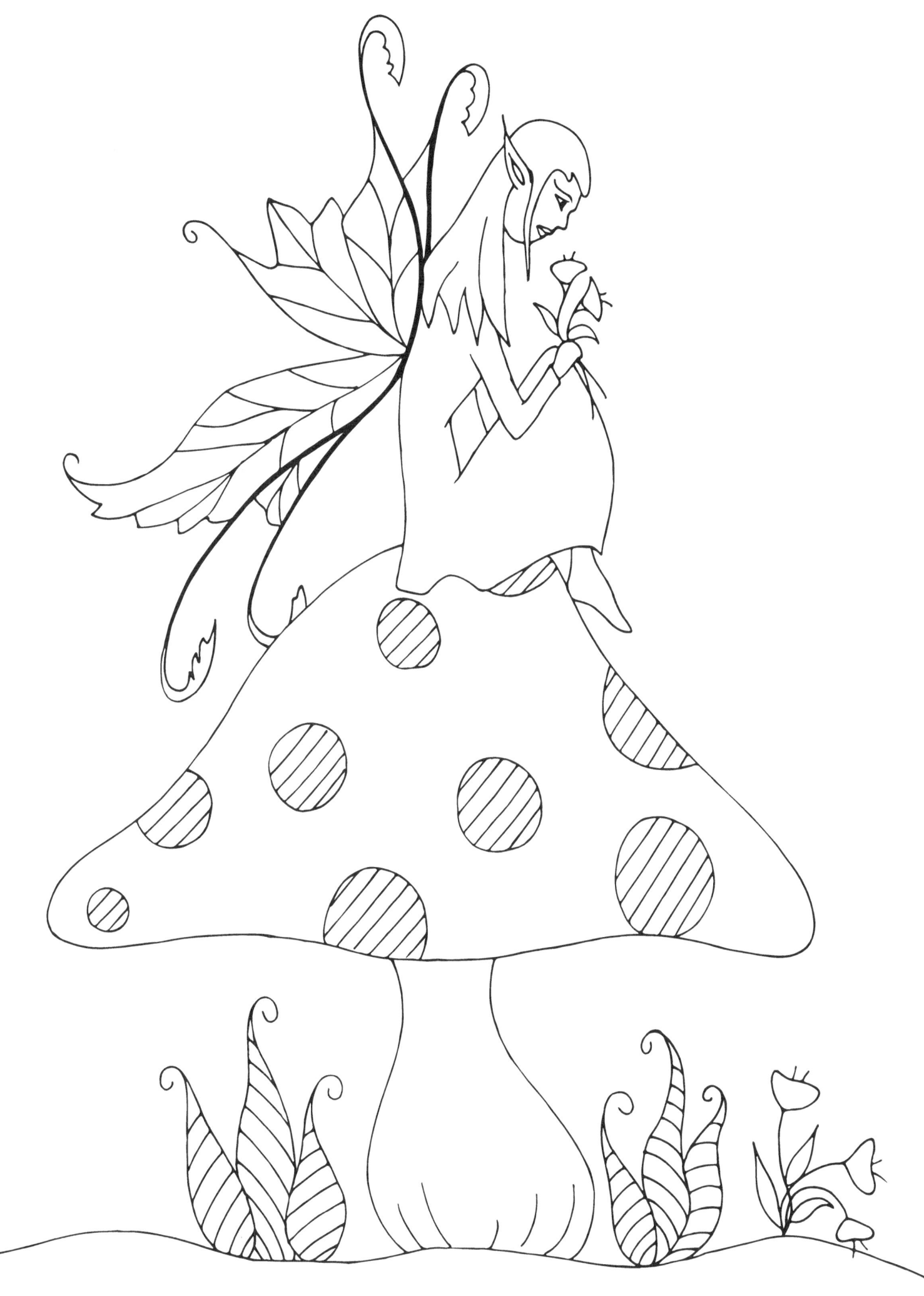

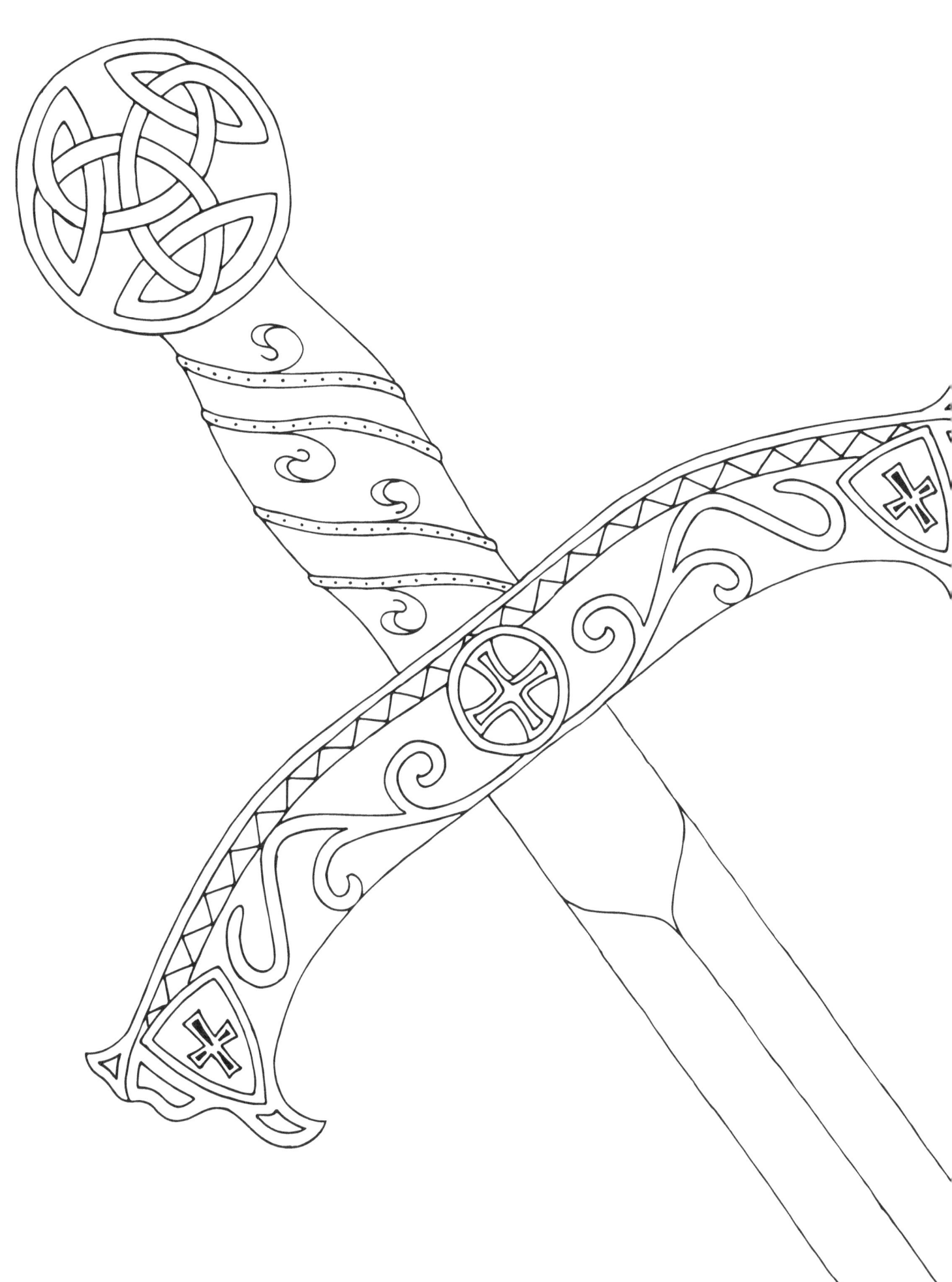

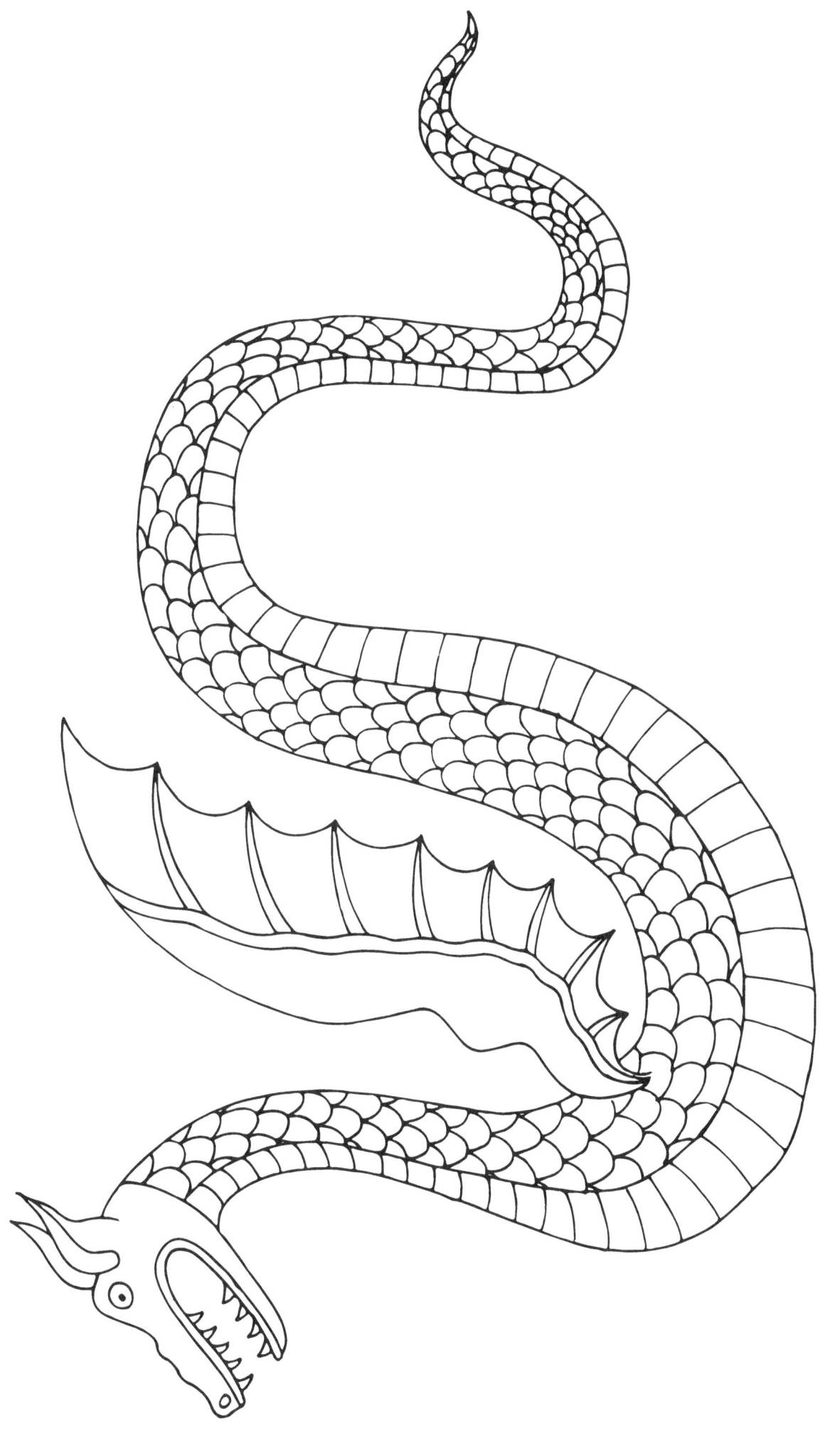

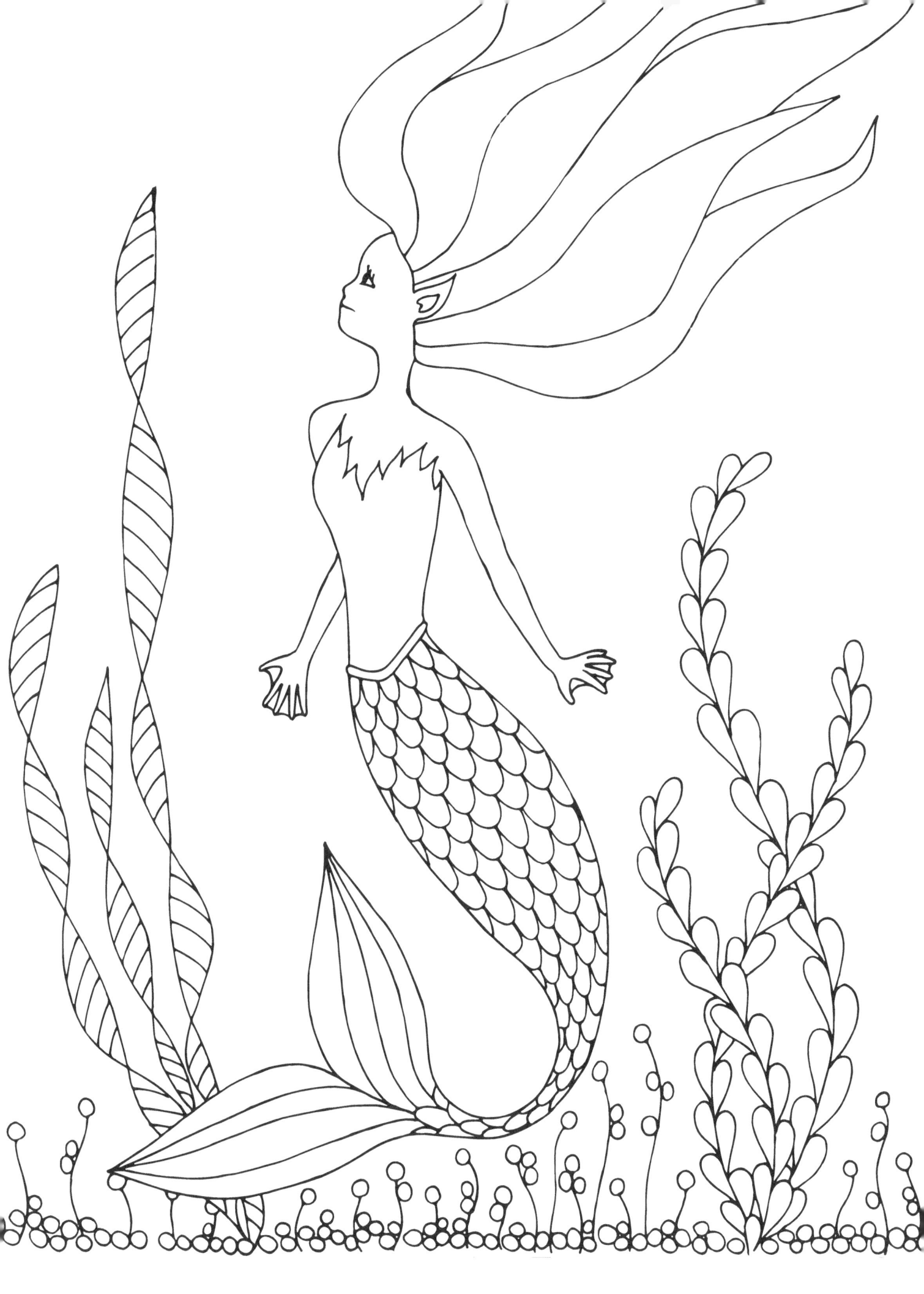

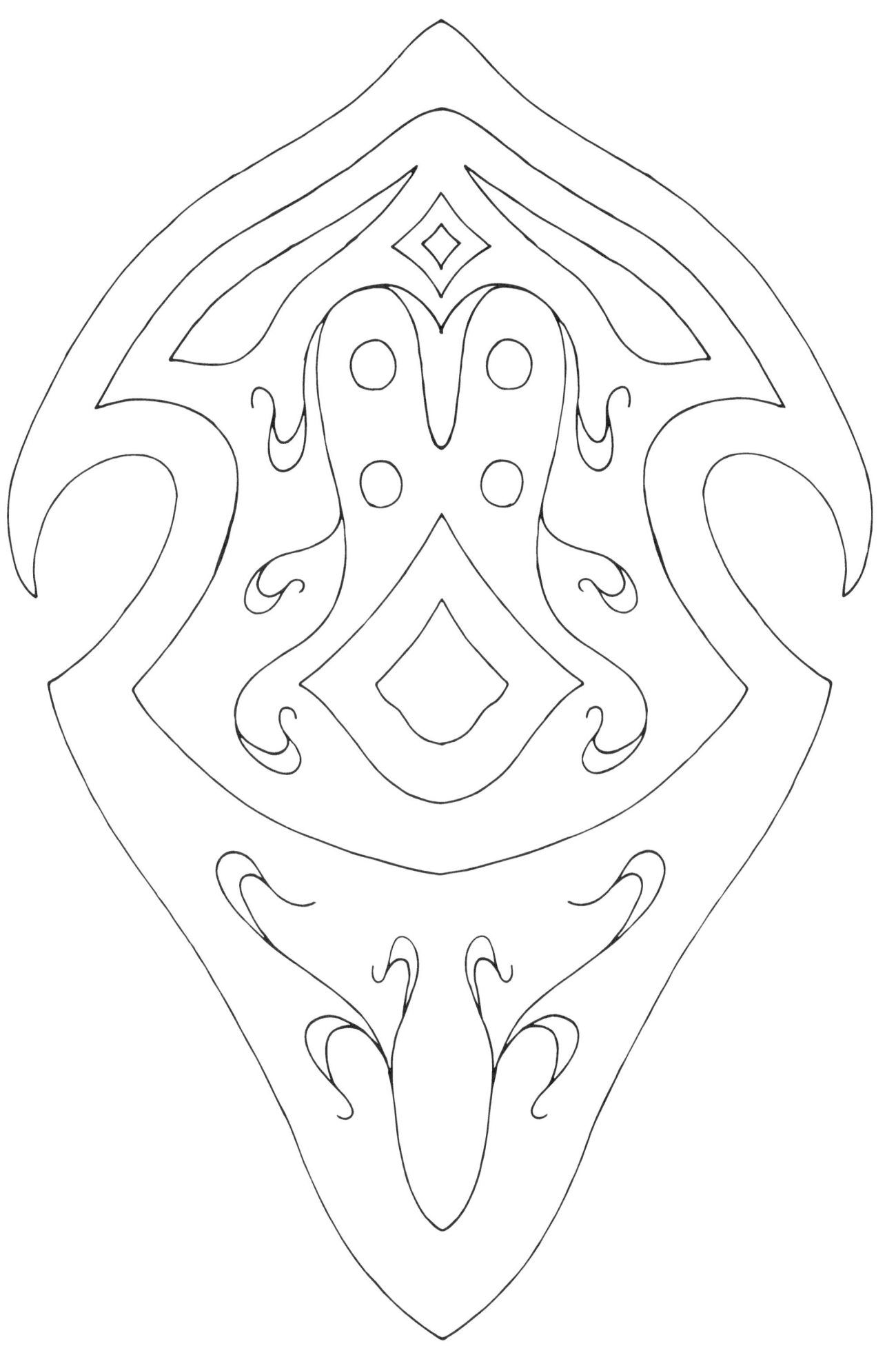

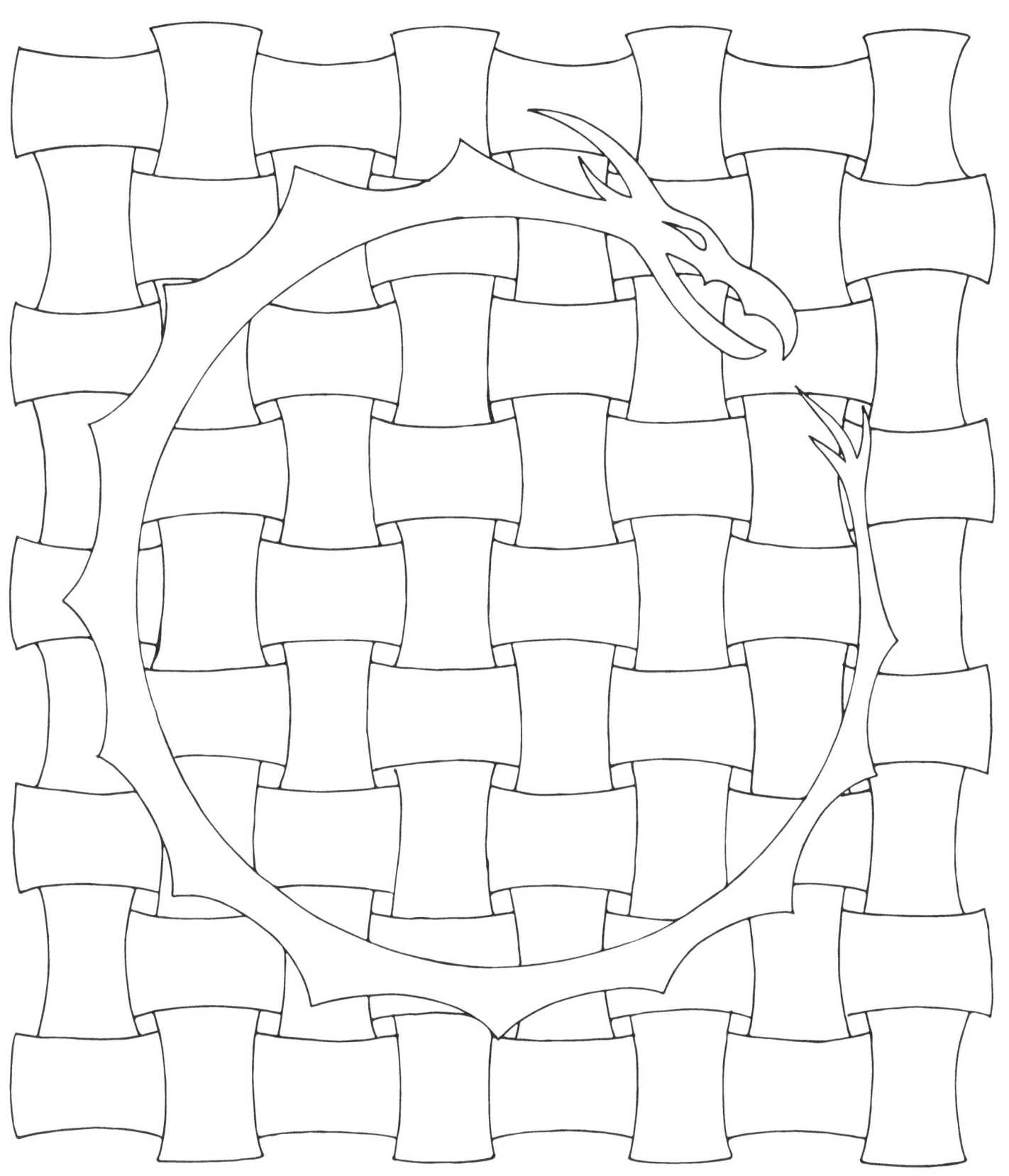

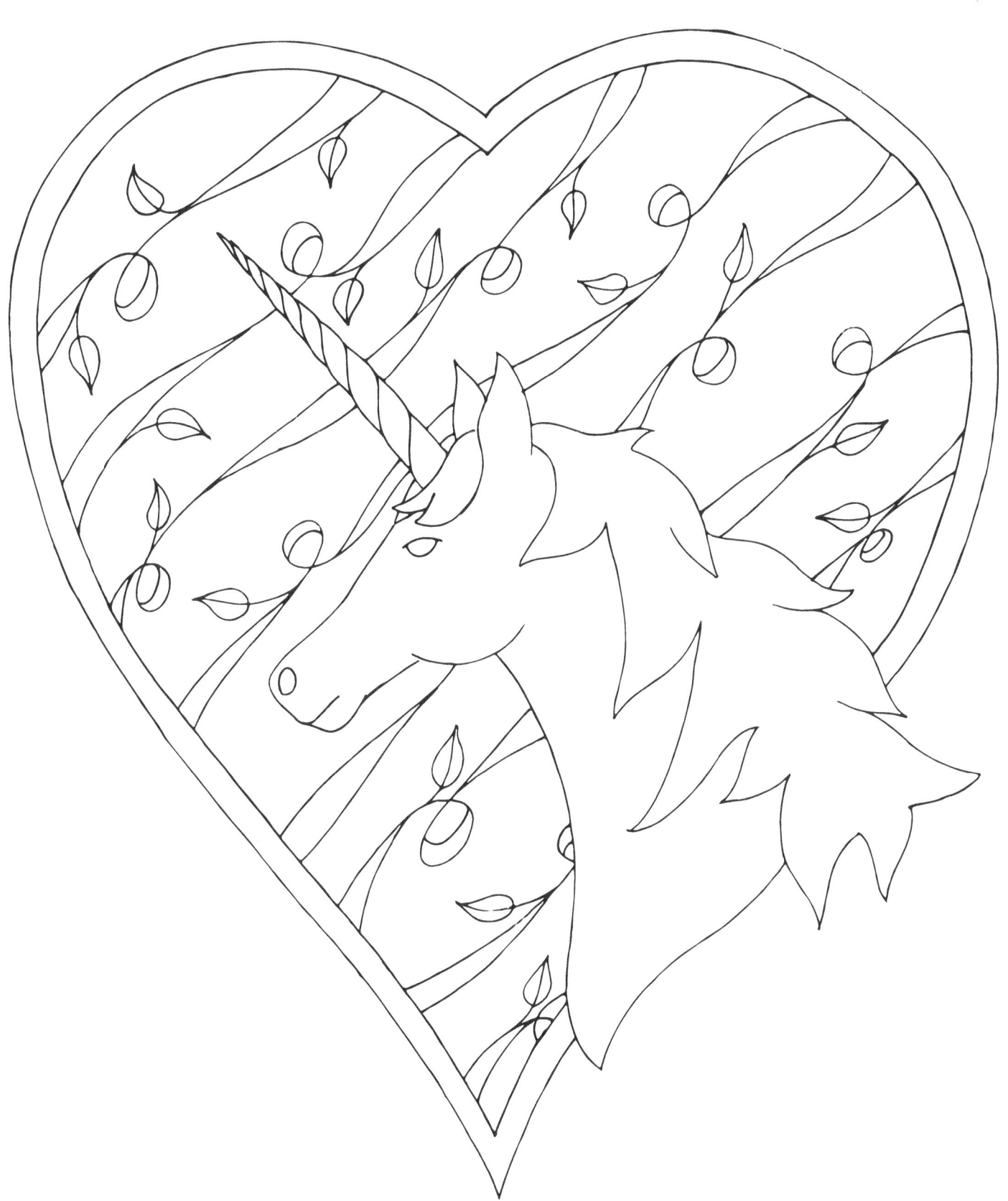

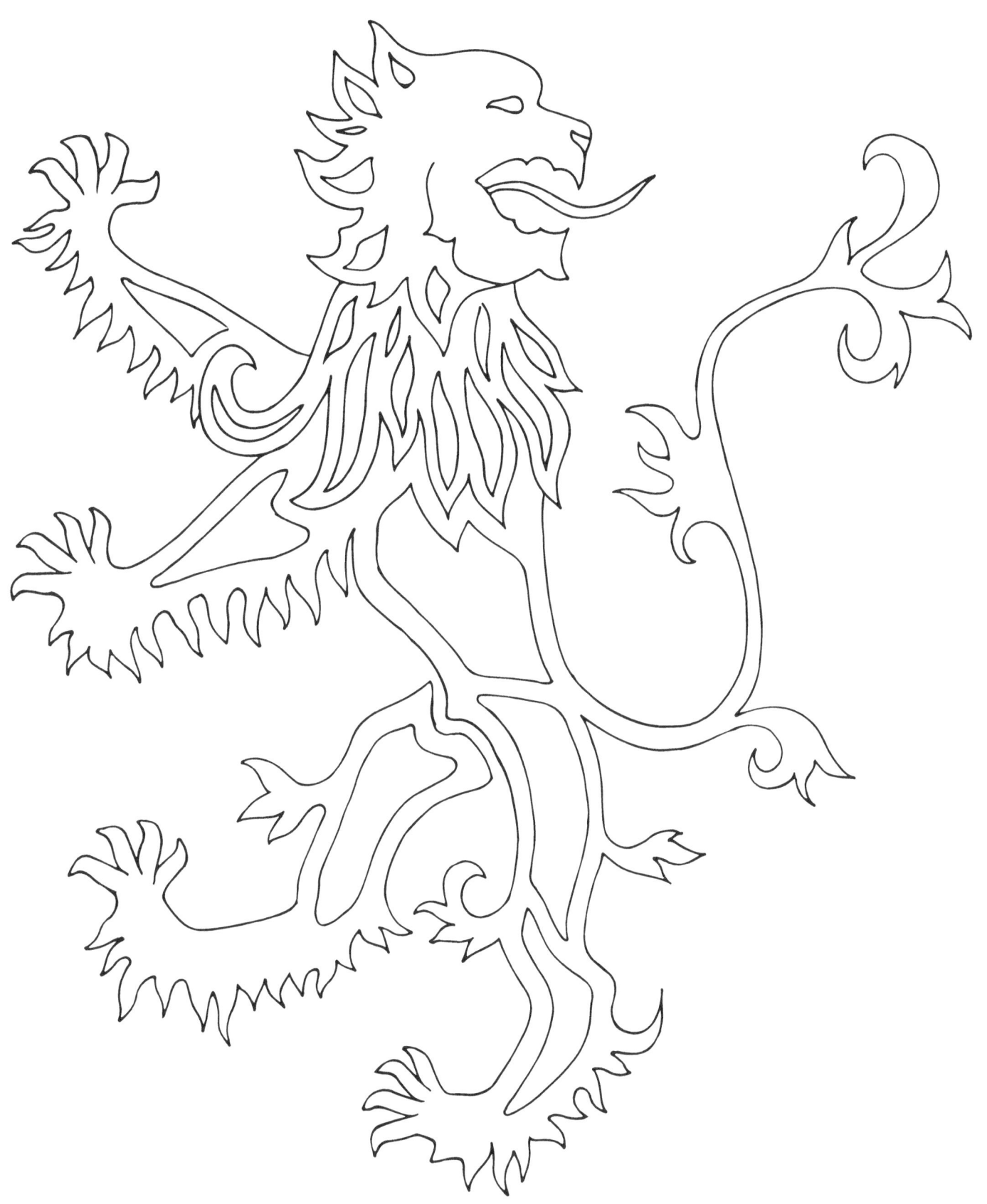

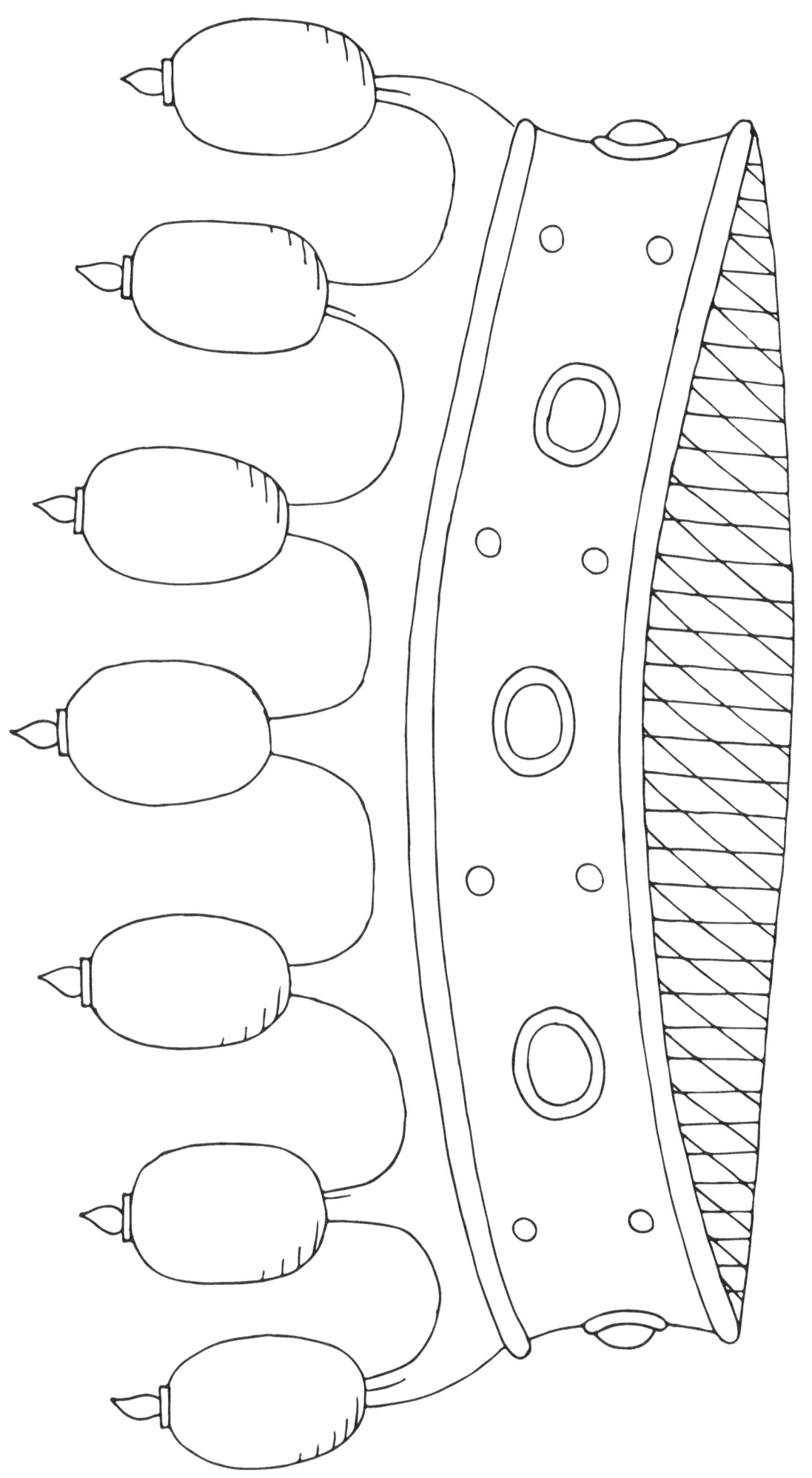

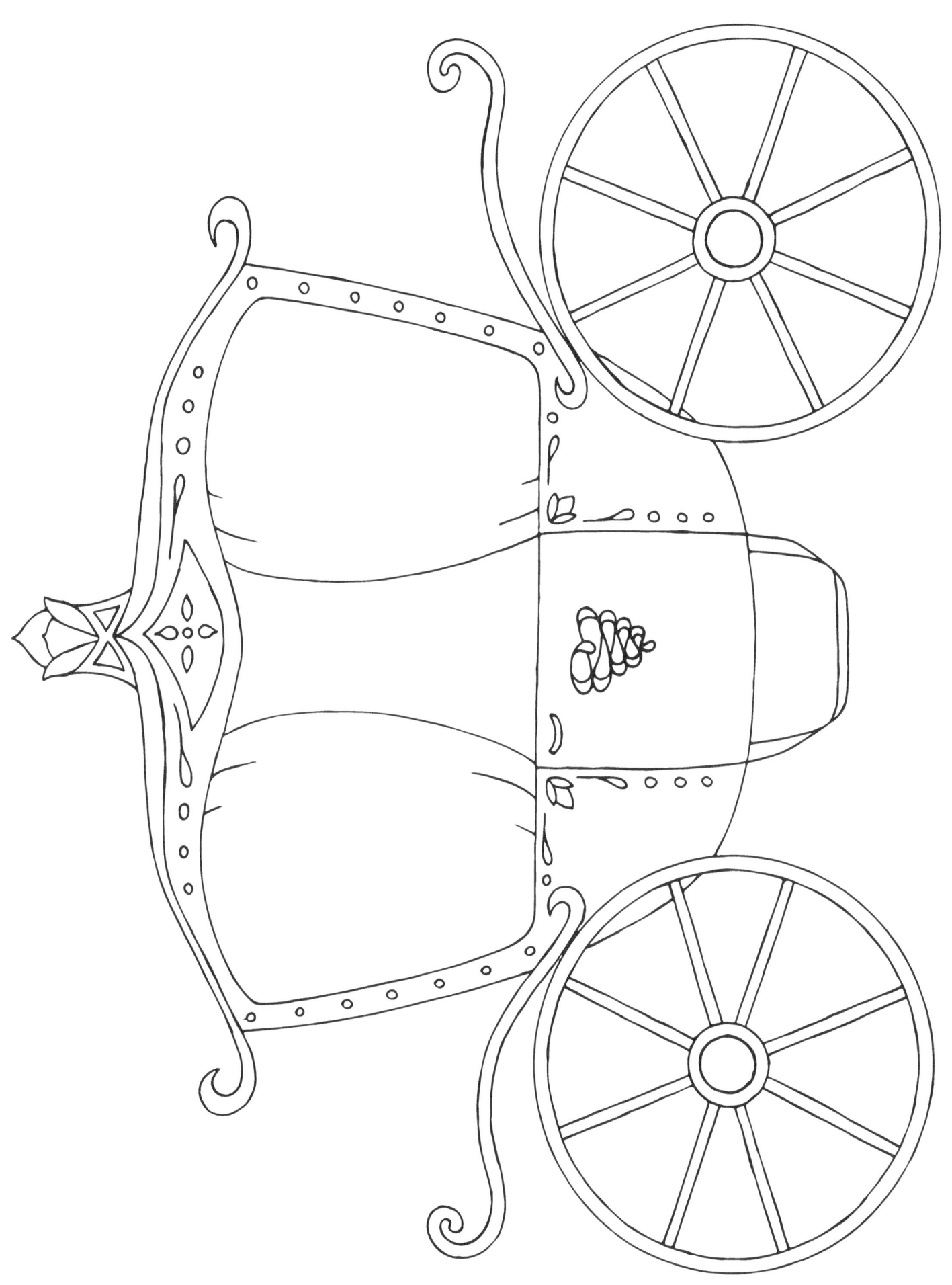

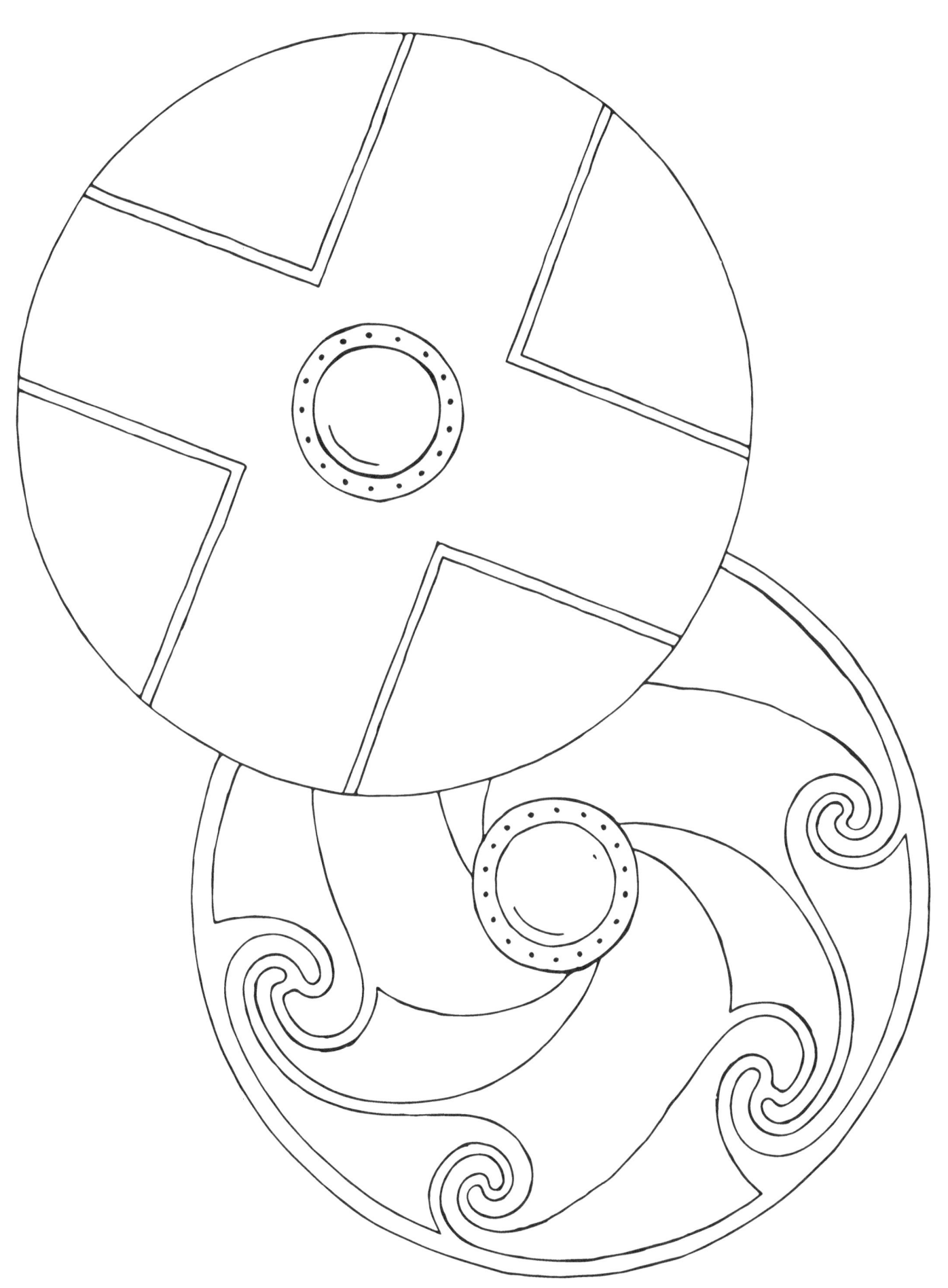

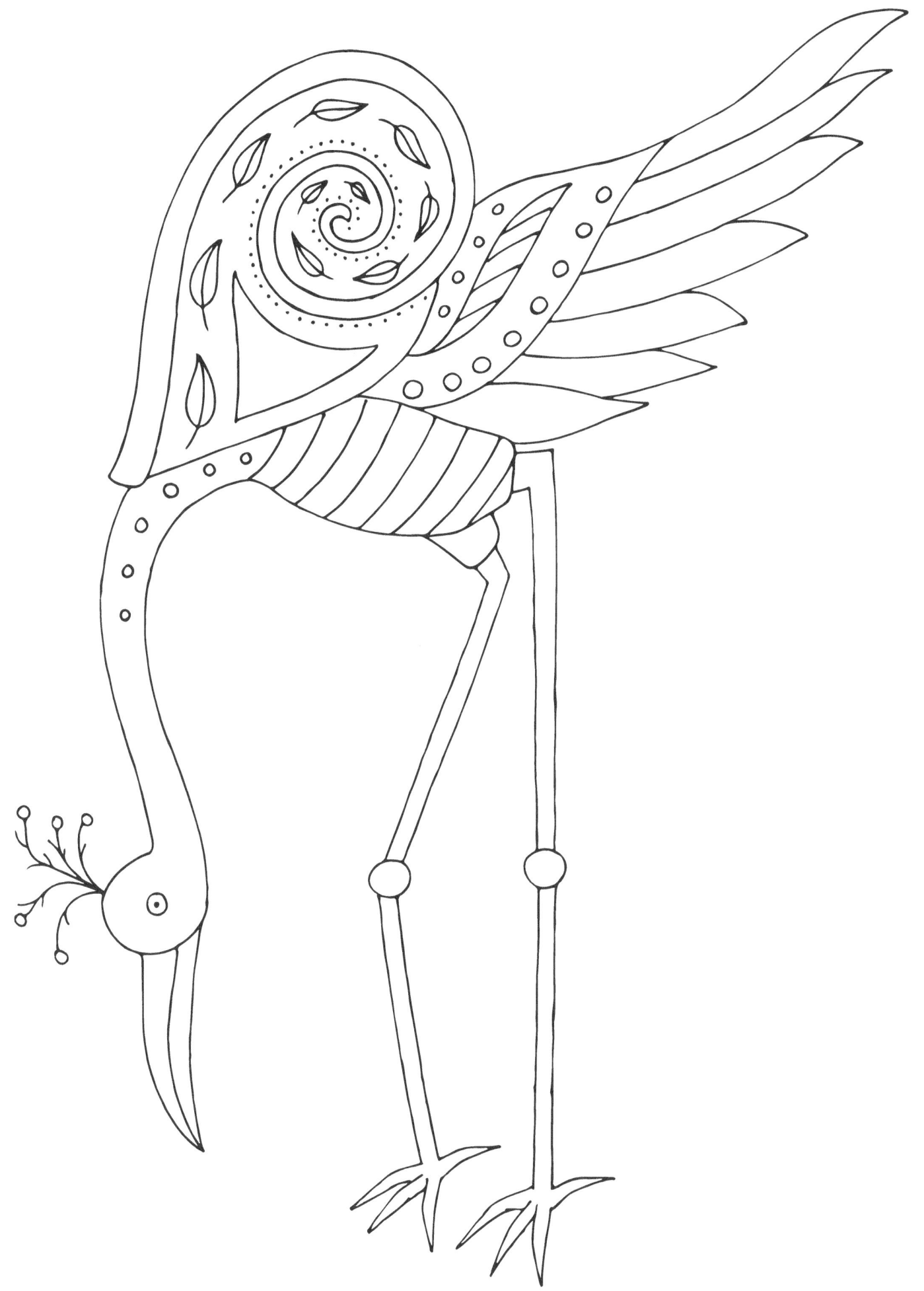

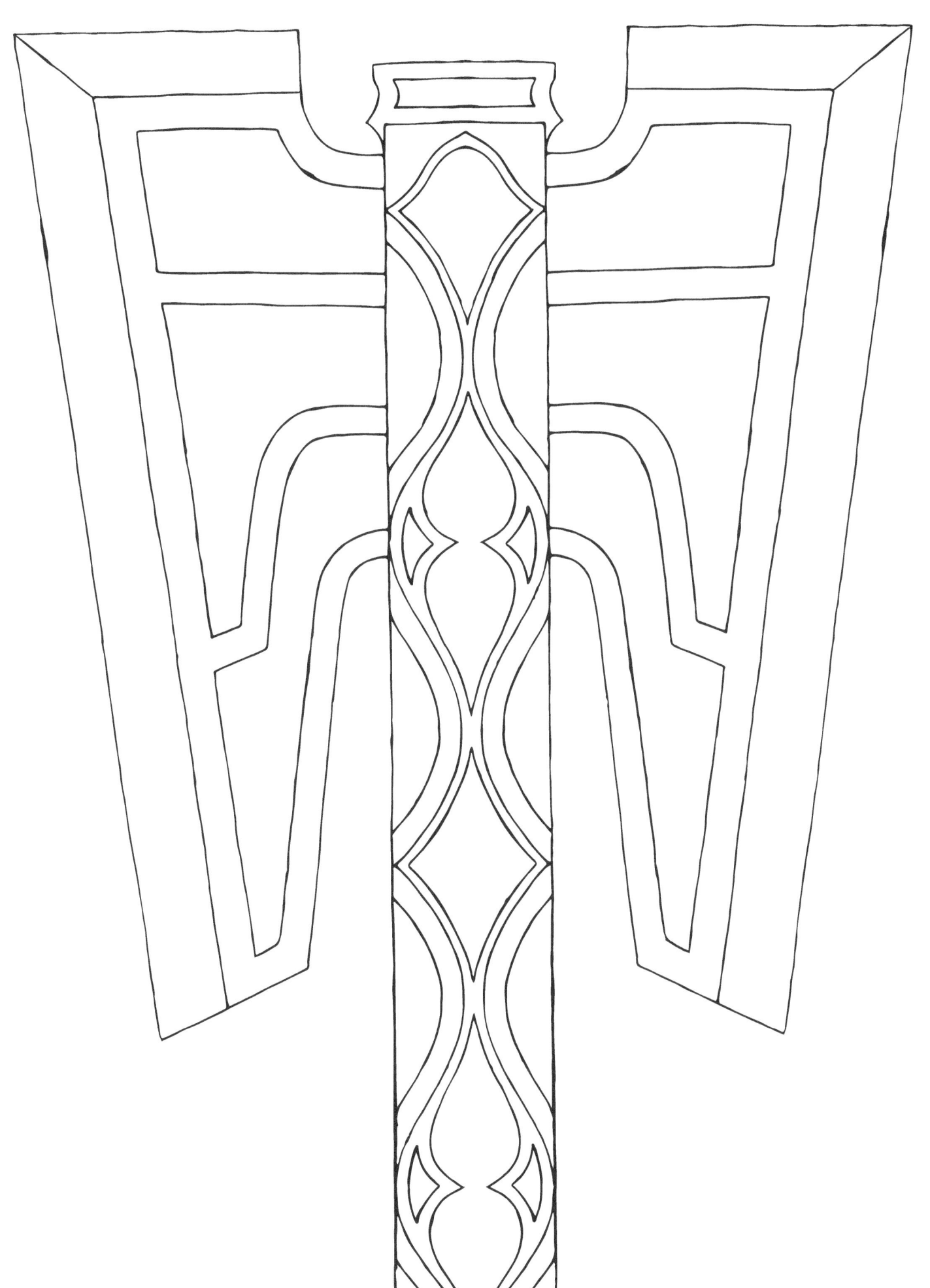

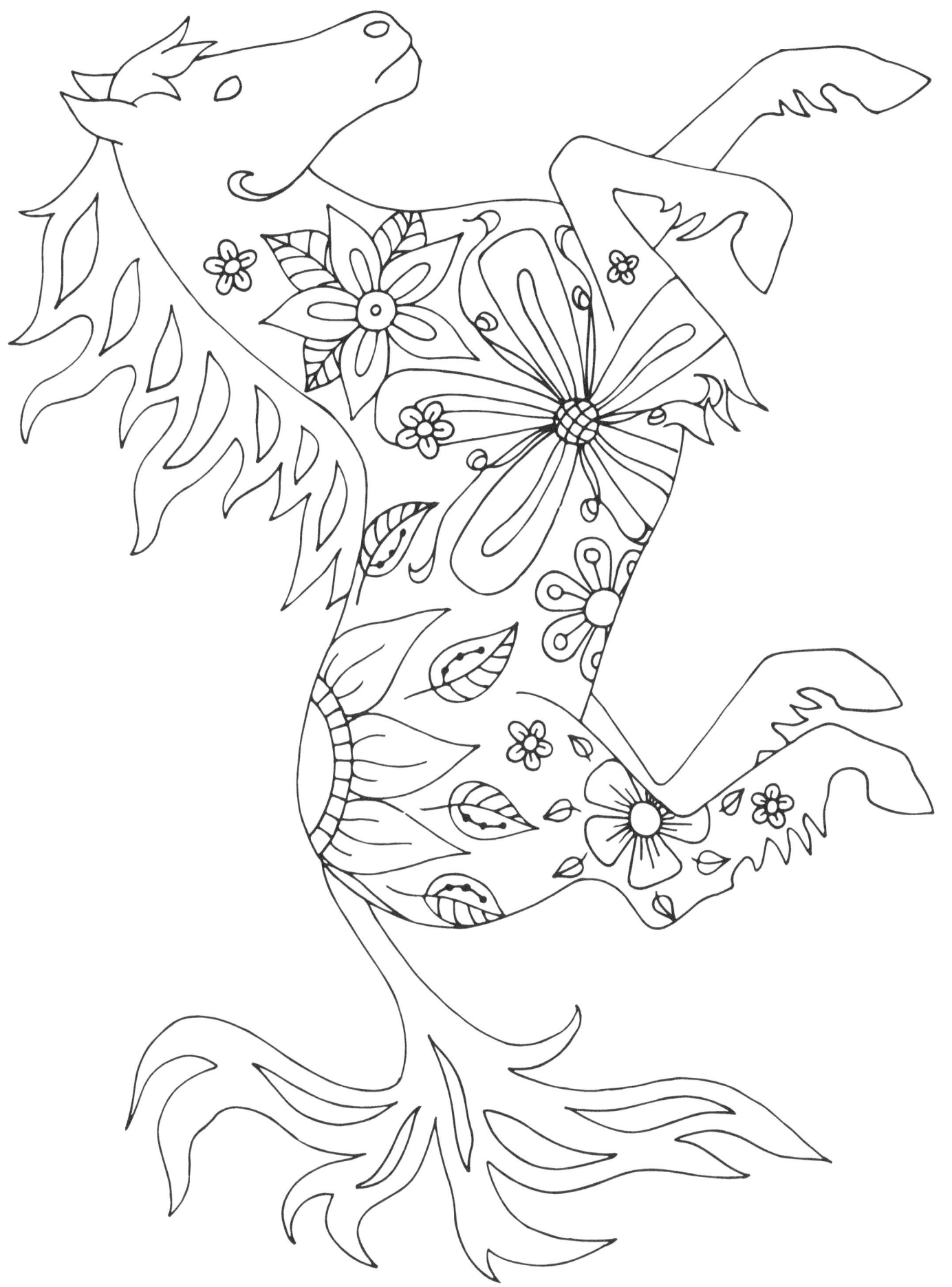

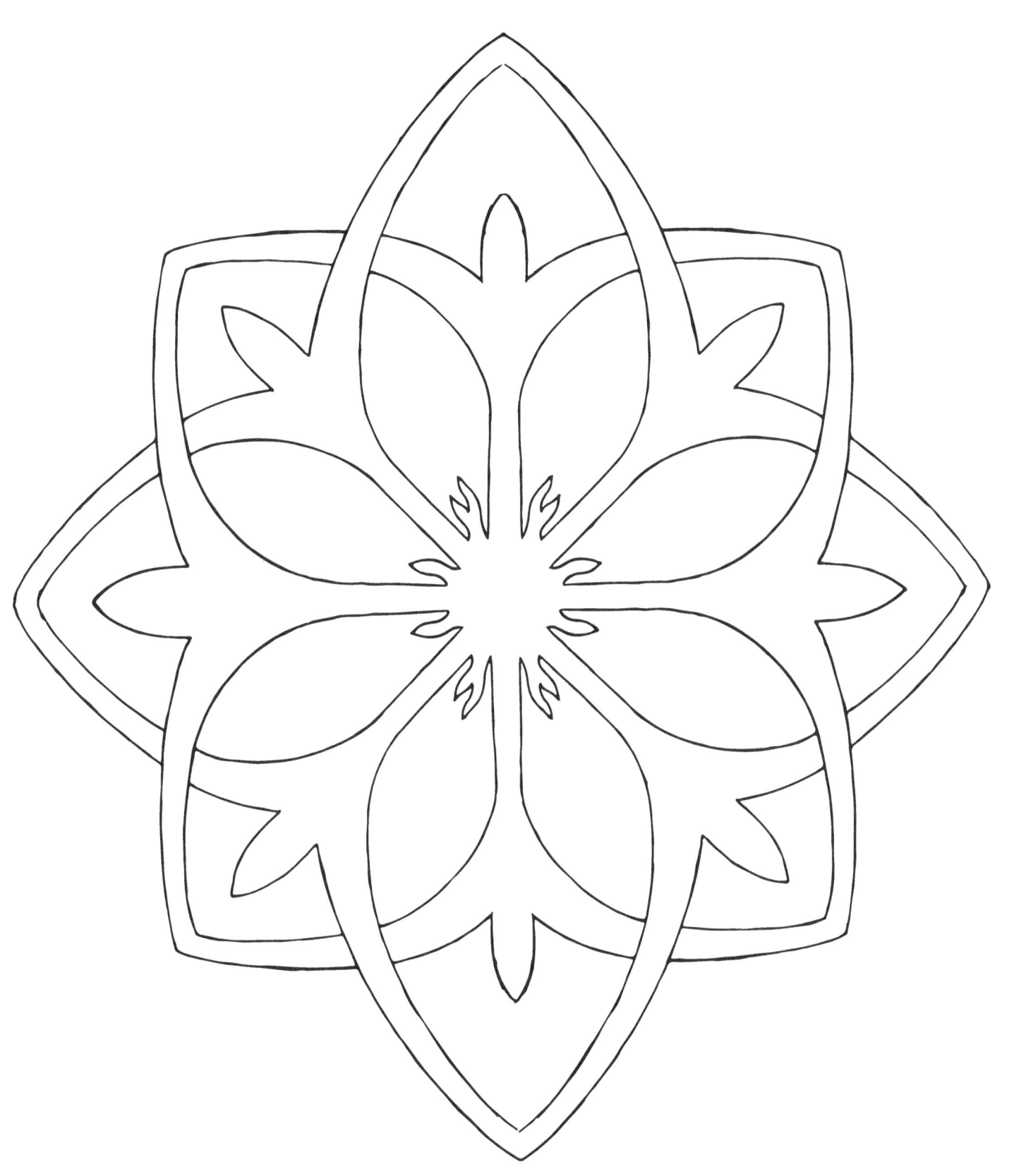

www.ingramcontent.com/pod-product-compliance
Lightning Source LLC
Chambersburg PA
CBHW080630190526
45169CB00009B/3343